STORIES THAT F*CKING MATTER

THREE PILLARS OF EPIC STORYTELLING TO DOMINATE MEDIA HEADLINES, WIN CLIENTS AND GROW YOUR BUSINESS

STEVEN LE VINE

GARRETT MCCLURE

Trigger Warning:

This book contains strong language (expletives) that may be upsetting to some readers.

CONTENTS

Foreword ix

Introduction xi

1. The Most Powerful Person in the World 1
2. Cutting Through The Noise 13
3. Stories That F*cking Matter™ 28
4. Roots: The Origin Story to Build Connection 46
5. Stakes: Level Of Risk, Investment, Or Sacrifice 56
6. Impact: Your Solution, Product, or Idea 72
7. Social Proof 85
8. Leverage Your Story to Make Headlines 93
9. Amplify Your Press Coverage 123
10. Becoming a Thought Leader 133
11. Advanced Storytelling Techniques 137

Conclusion 161
Afterword 163
Acknowledgments 169
References 173

This book is dedicated to all of the rule-breakers, risk-takers

and world-changers.

We are humbled by your passion and bravery to live your truth

and tell your stories.

— GARRETT & STEVEN

FOREWORD

Imagine a caveman hovering around a warm fire protecting them from the vicious animals surrounding them.

To make life more tolerable, our cave dwellers talk to each other about what happened on the hunt, their dreams, how they burned their fingers cooking, and what the baby said to the half-wolf, half-dog hanging around the fire.

These are the origins of storytelling.

It proceeded through the ages. Through the Greeks and their masterful playwrights, the Romans and their legends, the Egyptians and their hieroglyphics, and the history of books, theatre, and gossip—all of them storytelling.

It's how early humans communicated and how humans communicate even today. Storytelling is as essential to human culture as is the food we eat and the air we breathe.

This book tells us some stories of today. It's a lovely idea, and I know you will enjoy it.

William Shatner
Los Angeles, California
August 2022

Photo by Manfred Baumann

INTRODUCTION

Ordinary people and creators alike have a hard time focusing their attention and sharing stories. Modern media changes so fast and is incredibly fragmented. Countless entrepreneurs and experts waste their time and money posting to social media or emailing or calling reporters and producers whose numbers have been long disconnected, all without seeing any return on their investment. Many have stalled, while others have given up. Such is the nature of the beast that drives the modern world. How do you cut through the noise in such a heartless market? Strangely enough, the answer is "with heart."

The current media environment is frenzied and oversaturated with content. Many solopreneurs are left confused about how to gain credibility and exposure. You did your due diligence and created a powerful and effective product or service. But it all boils down to one question: *Does your story fucking matter if nobody hears it?*

The ever-elusive media can be a powerful ally in your search for new clients and business opportunities. But how do you win such an ally?

Creative solopreneurs with an established business sometimes face a growing and scaling challenge. Most likely, they are also a personal brand, such as the founder of a cosmetics brand, a performance coach, a professional motivational speaker, or an author of plant-based nutrition books. These niches are cutthroat, but developing your storytelling skills can make a noticeable difference. Everyone can tell a story, but not everyone knows how to tell a story that matters. If only someone could spill the beans!

Fortunately, you've got industry experts on your side, ready to share the secret formula for how to tell a *Story That Fucking Matters* and cut through the noise. Credibility, visibility, and media attention are all within reach. We'll guide you through these intimidating waters and elevate your understanding, teaching you how to:

- Gain confidence in how to craft and pitch a story.
- Understand what "noise" is and how to cut through it with authentic storytelling.
- Gain attention and exposure in the media that you rightfully deserve.

As Mr. Shatner explains, storytelling is as old as mankind itself. The art of storytelling is a primal force that can be used to connect with people or it can divide the masses; it all depends on how a story is told.

When you learn to master the art of storytelling, people will notice.

A well-crafted story will gain and guide the audience's attention. Storytelling creates a foundation of trust with your target audience, but so many entrepreneurs and experts are not capitalizing on this learned skill.

This is why we have poured our extensive knowledge into this book.

We wanted to provide you with a roadmap to hone your skills, empowering you to tell stories that fucking matter. No more drowning in a sea of noise!

Trying new things and finding innovative ways of moving forward should be the creed of every entrepreneur. Throughout my life, I have fearlessly chased new experiences, even relocating across the country, constantly seeking fresh ways to develop and grow. Every mile I traveled and every person I met added to the story of my life and the story I've crafted (and continue to hone) for business success.

How can you achieve more, reach your target market, and grow both professionally and personally?

It all boils down to telling a story that really fucking matters. Now is your time to shine and tell your own story. And with this book, we're going to help make it easy for you!

A Quick Overview of This Book

This book is organized into 4 sections:

Storytelling & Noise: A Brief History of Media's Rise to Dominate Our Collective Story

In this section, we lay the groundwork to give you a clear understanding of the power of a story. We also provide important context to illustrate how modern media has harnessed storytelling to impact our everyday lives.

The Stories That F*cking Matter™ Model

Here we break down the three core pillars to create your story that fucking matters—a story that breaks through all the noise to get you seen and heard. In these pages, you'll learn how to expertly craft a compelling story around the key elements of *Roots*, *Stakes*, and *Impact*.

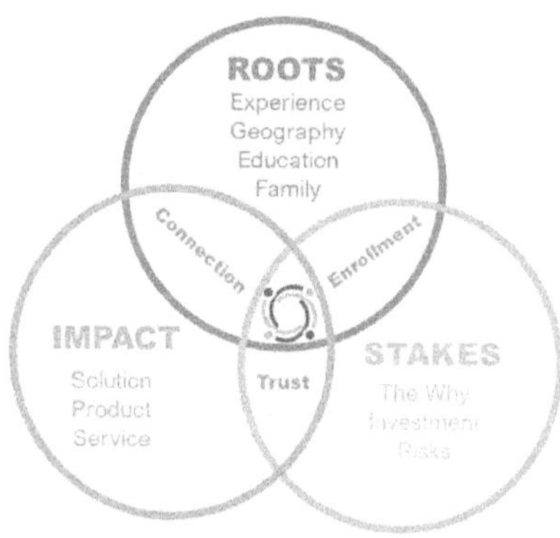

The Stories That F*cking Matter™ Model

Getting Press: Leveraging Your Story to Win Hearts & Headlines

Armed with a story that fucking matters, we lay out the simple steps to get your story told and broadcast by the media. We are passionate about powerful stories that have a positive impact in our world. So, we are pulling back the curtain to help more authentic and compelling stories make it into the headlines.

Advanced Techniques and Tips

Once you have a well-crafted story or perhaps even some great press coverage, you aren't done yet. Keep reading to find a few more tips and insider tricks to maximize your coverage and perhaps even go viral.

This book has been a work of passion, and we are dedicated to helping you tell great stories that will help you grow your brand or business, or advance your mission. While on this journey to create this book, it has been an honor to work with some incredibly talented people who we are grateful to call both clients and friends.

As you make your way through this book, visit our website for more resources and to join the community:

www.StoriesMatterBook.com

1

THE MOST POWERFUL PERSON IN THE WORLD

The most powerful person in the world is the storyteller. The storyteller sets the vision, values, and agenda of an entire generation that is to come.

— STEVE JOBS

Stories are the most powerful tool in human existence! Storytelling is one of the oldest skills humankind has developed. How you leverage this power to create your truth, to tell your story, is entirely up to you.

Steve Jobs was a master storyteller. He used this world-class talent to capture the hearts (and wallets) of millions of people year after year. Later in Chapter 3, we'll show you exactly how to apply the principles of a Story That Fucking Matters or STFM to your own brand, similar to how Jobs weaved one around Apple and its products.

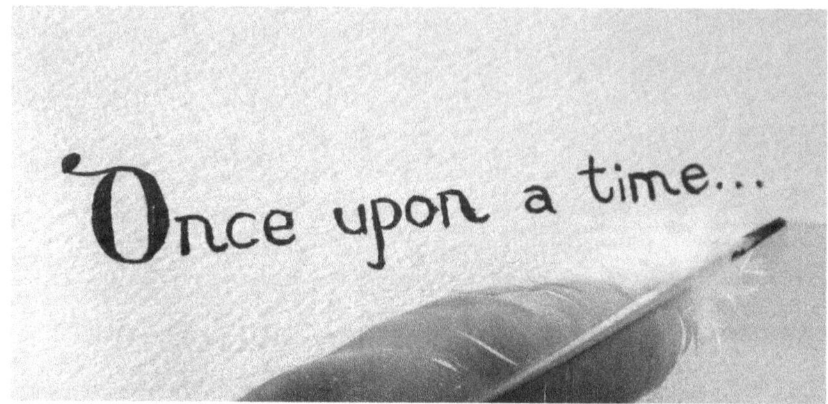

But for now, consider this, Apple's products consistently cost more than their competitors, are less customizable, and often offer fewer integrations and interoperability. But the story around the beauty and ease-of-use supplants all those facts just stated. (Truth be told - I'm a total Apple fanboy too. I even adopted and hold dear the story "Think Differently" - an Apple advertising slogan from the 1990s.)

In reality, facts and truth are completely subjective—and easily manipulated by a well-crafted story.

> **Truth is subjective.**
> Every moment of every day each individual is deciding what's real and what's not for themselves. And we are all doing it both internally and externally.

Think about the story of yourself. Who are you?

Most likely, you identify as a Man or Woman, or perhaps you're non-binary and have chosen a completely different path to interpret your story of *self*. But regardless, you have an internal story about who you are, what you stand for, and what you value.

Marketers and advertisers, such as Apple's Jobs, have tapped into these stories to create powerful associations with their products. Apple created a whole fan base and captured audiences worldwide with a simple slogan: "Think Differently." And the associated creative was full of stunning images of a product that focused on beautiful, sleek design and intuitive interfaces. A dramatic shift from the Microsoft world of spreadsheets, technical specs, and hard lines.

And in that stroke of genius, a brand was born and solidified its place in the world.

Bear in mind that once perceptions and first impressions are formed, they are remarkably persistent, as Stanford researchers discovered in 1975 (Kolbert, 2017). So go about telling your truth carefully or risk becoming someone's redemption story, as is the case with Anna Sorokin.

Stories Create Reality

A real news article inspired the 2022 Netflix series, *Inventing Anna*. Two women in this tale knew how to wield the power of stories.

In real life, Jessica Pressler was a journalist determined to redeem herself after a mistake threatened to end her career (Nugent, 2022). Anna Sorokin did not heed the wisdom in Jobs' words and utilized her talent for storytelling to live her best life as someone else, committing fraud and grand larceny in the process. While Pressler undoubtedly got the redemption she sought, it was Anna Sorokin who had the world fixated on one question: *How the fuck did she do that?*

Every successful story demands something that can't be bought—time.

Neffatari Davis, the 25-year-old concierge at the luxury hotel 11 Howard, realized this early on when dealing with Sorokin. "This is not a guest that needs my help. This is a guest that wants my time," the young concierge revealed (Pressler, 2022). By commanding the time of others, Sorokin used storytelling to weave a new reality. In that reality, she was Anna Delvey, a German socialite and heiress whose fanciful storytelling allowed everyone to draw their own conclusions. It was a potent recipe. Through her narrative and people's hardwired response to hold on to perceptions, Sorokin was able to keep the ruse going until it came undone at the seams.

The Twin Weapons of Narrative and Reinforcement

Stories have importance beyond simple interpersonal communication. They are powerful drivers of the economy and can have consequences on a global scale.

In the presidential address to the American Economic Association, Nobel Laureate Bob Shiller drew attention to the power of storytelling. He pointed out that the simpler a story is, the more persuasive it becomes since it agrees with our own preconceptions (Markey-Towler, 2017).

This is pretty much what Sorokin did. She created an agreeable enough narrative that played on the preconceptions people may have held about trust fund babies, earning *their* trust along the way. When we apply this concept of a simple, agreeable narrative to the economy as a whole, we discover something more—our expectations shape our behavior.

The simpler a story is, the more it becomes embedded in one's mind, shaping others' expectations. Sorokin's simple story of being a "trust fund baby" certainly molded the expectations of those she interacted with (handing out crisp $100 bills like candy reinforced those expecta-tions). Using the twin weapons of simple narrative and positive rein-forcement, Sorokin was able to get away with her antics for a considerable while. But positive reinforcement doesn't have to take the form of handing out greenbacks!

Think of positive reinforcement as rewarding the behavior you want to encourage. Businesses use this all the time to encourage consumers to buy their products. Special offers, prizes, and promotions are all forms of positive reinforcement that encourage consumers to purchase certain products or use certain services.

Let's apply this concept of narrative and positive reinforcement to the entrepreneur. Chances are, an investor will act more readily if the founder of a kickass kombucha brand manages to embed a positive narrative in the minds of potential investors about the brand.

Positive stories translate into expectations of future returns in the financial market, which serves as positive reinforcement for investors. This is why stories make up one of the pillars that support the surges in financial sectors such as the stock market. It creates an expectation and then rewards that expectation.

Narrative and the Liquidity Trap

Without a positive narrative, strong expectations of future returns can't be formed and rewarded. No amount of cheap credit can entice growth in a business if its story is uninspiring. This is the infamous liquidity trap.

A compelling story, one that is simple and agrees with preconceptions, is a powerful tool to help overcome the liquidity trap. It is a tool that Sorokin, for better or worse, used sublimely. A simple story sticks. When combined with emotionally charged ideas, they can become embedded in the minds of your target audience and inform expectations.

Let's explore a consumer packaged goods brand under two different narratives.

> *Narrative One*: "Our product uses all-natural ingredients and is packed with real-life health benefits that empower people to perform at and feel their best!"

> *Narrative Two*: "Our product is the cheapest."

Which narrative do you think creates a better expectation of future returns? The obvious answer is "Narrative One." It creates a powerful story that plays on our notions of emotionally charged concepts: All-natural products, health empowerment, and enhancing one's daily performance. Similarly, a lifestyle coach, motivational speaker, or author of a book on biohacking will have little success if their stories are not compelling and emotionally charged.

Financial history is rich with examples pointing to the power of storytelling. Few historical narratives stick as persistently in the American consciousness as the Great Depression (John Kenneth Galbraith, 1975). Most point to the 1929 stock market crash as the starting point.

That event alone influenced America's preconceptions of future returns, painting a dismal picture. In turn, this reduced consumer spending, stifled investment, and caused a steep decline in economic activity. In short, it created a massive liquidity trap for the United States.

Yet another example from the annals of history can be found in Louisiana when King Louis XV granted the Mississippi Company the profits of the colony. This action led to the share value of the Mississippi Company rising so high that it jump started the stagnant French economy! Using pamphlets, cartoons, and posters, a narrative of uncurbed wealth spread, stimulating the company's growth even more.

Those are the two extremes on the continuum of success that a powerful narrative can stimulate: stupendous success or utter destruction. If you are not careful, your storytelling can come back to bite you in the ass, just like it did with Anna Sorokin.

Changing the Story

Cryptocurrencies are a unique and modern example of the power of changing narratives. Storytelling here plays an interesting balancing and filtering role. While this trait is not unique to the crypto world, it is certainly easy to observe here. Let's elaborate on this concept.

The possibility of becoming a crypto millionaire is an enticing lure for many future-forward investors, and it paints a picture of handsome returns as a reward for risk. It is a narrative that appeals to early adopters and those with a high tolerance for risk. A positive outlook and story are dominant in these individuals' minds.

At the same time, this highly speculative market dissuades individuals who have a low-risk appetite from venturing into these digital waters. Here, the negative narrative of loss, scams, and market volatility screams the loudest.

Of course, the general narrative of crypto is changing daily. With the rise of the metaverse and NFTs (non-fungible tokens), crypto's story is changing from an elusive and thrilling pastime to something more functional.

As a nascent sector, it is still refining its own narrative, which is why we find everything from scandals to the incredibly cute antics of the late Mr. Goxx, the cryptocurrency trading hamster (yes, you read that right), woven into the fabric of the crypto story.

When Technology Becomes the Storyteller: The Russia-Ukraine War

Technology has played a major role around the narrative of the Russia-Ukraine War. The story about the war (or "special military operation" if you're within the Russian Federation) has continuously changed depending on which side of the border you find yourself on. War is abhorrent, and it is our sincerest hope that humanity can evolve beyond its base and conflict-driven nature.

Have you ever heard the advice that you can dilute bad press with tons of good press? It is flawed advice that will leave a hole in your pocket. As Warren Buffet notes, it takes a long time to build a reputation but only five minutes to destroy it.

The negativity bias is the reason good reputations can be wiped out in a matter of minutes, and why you should call BS on the technique of "good press dilution."

As for P.T. Barnum's famous quote, "There's no such thing as bad publicity," just take a look at the court case of *Amber Heard vs. Johnny Depp*. She will likely never live the "chocolate factory" moment down.

Negativity bias is our innate proclivity to pay more attention to negative information than positive information. Think of it as a lopsided way in which negative and positive occurrences are processed (Moore, 2019). Negative events elicit a stronger and faster response, which explains why we tend to dwell on insults. Yes, you can thank the negativity bias for those true crime binges as well. The negativity bias draws our attention to one side of a story, leading us to ruminate over small things or fret over a bad impression. Psychologists believe that negativity bias may be an adaptive function of evolution to protect us from potentially harmful stimuli in a harsh world.

Your audience or market can be your biggest advocates or your biggest detractors. It all depends on the narrative. In the case of the Russia-Ukraine war, bad press breeds more bad press, creating a fertile ground for story suppression and misinformation. You can see how the negativity bias runs rampant.

The Russia-Ukraine war is a war on truth. "Truth," as we learned earlier, is highly subjective. A fair amount of mud-slinging is happening on all sides of the wartime border.

Amid the ongoing news stories, photos and videos populate search feeds using powerful information as weapons of warfare. Social media makes it especially easy for fake news to spread (a phenomenon we observed throughout the coronavirus pandemic and recent national

U.S. elections). However, media outlets, news websites, and good ol' television are still some of the go-to news sources for many individuals, which means these information sources play a big role in spreading dis- and misinformation (Lameiras, 2022).

In Russia, more than half of the population (54%) still trusts television over other media as their primary news source (Levada Center, 2022). This number has increased by a staggering 10 percentage points since the invasion of Ukraine began. Two of the three main channels are majority-owned by the state, making them convenient vehicles to spread one viewpoint on the war, i.e., a narrative that the war was necessary. Only 17% of the population gets their news from online sources. This is a good example of how the story is being controlled on a large scale to spread a particular subjective "truth."

This phenomenon is not unique to Russia. State-owned media in South Africa earned the moniker "Sunshine News," an ironic name that points to the outlet's strategy to stifle editorial independence with positive news stories. The point is that if you control the narrative, you essentially control the heart of the people. Remember, the narrative informs expectations and, by extension, behavior.

The Polarizing Role of Social Media

We can thank the negativity bias once again for the rapid spread of polarizing and hateful content on social media. Technology makes it much easier to hate on others anonymously, and troll factories go about their business in creative and deceptive ways. This has prompted a new strategy to surface—enticing people to share messages through comments and shares using their original profiles. The social media algorithms register this activity as organic, and the content stays.

Consequently, TikTok and Twitter pro-war accounts increased their number of followers by thousands over a few days. This led to Twitter removing thousands of accounts and pieces of content that violated their spam policies.

TikTok is blocked in several countries, including Russia, but users can still access their accounts through the web version of the app using a VPN. Journalists and fact-checkers have a hard time debunking false-hoods as increasingly advanced technologies are employed to spread a particular narrative. We'll highlight some examples.

Deepfakes: March 16th, 2022, two deepfakes appeared on Twitter that supposedly showed the Ukrainian and Russian presidents announcing the surrender of Kyiv. These videos were made using deepfake technology. It is often near-impossible to tell whether a video is the real deal or a deepfake at first glance, and it can erode trust in the target population.

Out-of-Context Content: Videos and images are often used out of context to further a particular narrative, depending on the sender of the message. Some images claim to depict Russian fighter jets being shot down or Ukrainian citizens ducking for cover. Some of these images are real images of war, while others have been lurking on the internet for years (Seitz & Klepper, 2022).

Live Streams: Undoubtedly, most of us saw live streams popping up all over the place at the start of the war. On TikTok, several accounts have been spotted broadcasting fake footage on a loop with dubbed sounds. Often this content has nothing to do with what is really happening in the war.

Ultra-Realistic Content: Advances in technology have given us super-realistic video games and special effects in films. Unfortunately, these near-real bits of content have been exploited to tell a distorted story of what is happening in Ukraine. A scene from *War of Chimeras*, a 2017 film directed by Anastasiia Starozhitska and Mariia Starozhitska, was shared thousands of times. This scene depicted an emotional scene of soldiers bidding their loved ones farewell before leaving for the war.

In the end, the war in Ukraine shows that the truth is highly subjective, and unscrupulous individuals can and will use technology to spread their narrative. Technology is useful for spreading a story, but it can quickly turn into mud-slinging if the content is extremely polarizing. These are all things worth considering when weaving your story. Stories have been passed down for thousands of years and impact every facet of our lives.

So, what impact do these stories have on your own life today? And how can you best leverage that power to your advantage?

2

CUTTING THROUGH THE NOISE

The crisp kiss of cool air slowly drags you from a deep and restful sleep. It is 6:15 a.m., and the iPhone is buzzing like crazy. You reach out to kill the alarm and then check the latest updates on your feeds.

It's a daily ritual of confronting a sea of red notification dots as you hop between your favorite apps. Keeping up with the trends and breaking news is starting to feel like work.

It is 7 a.m. now. You've had your fill of app-hopping for the time being. It is so hard to tell what is attention-worthy these days. Every platform seems to be screaming for your attention—the bright, flashing lights, the smooth color palette, the ding of another push notification. Every story tugs on the frayed strings of your unraveling attention. The reality is that today's media landscape is fragmented with booming echo chambers. The attention economy is competing for your most precious resource—your time.

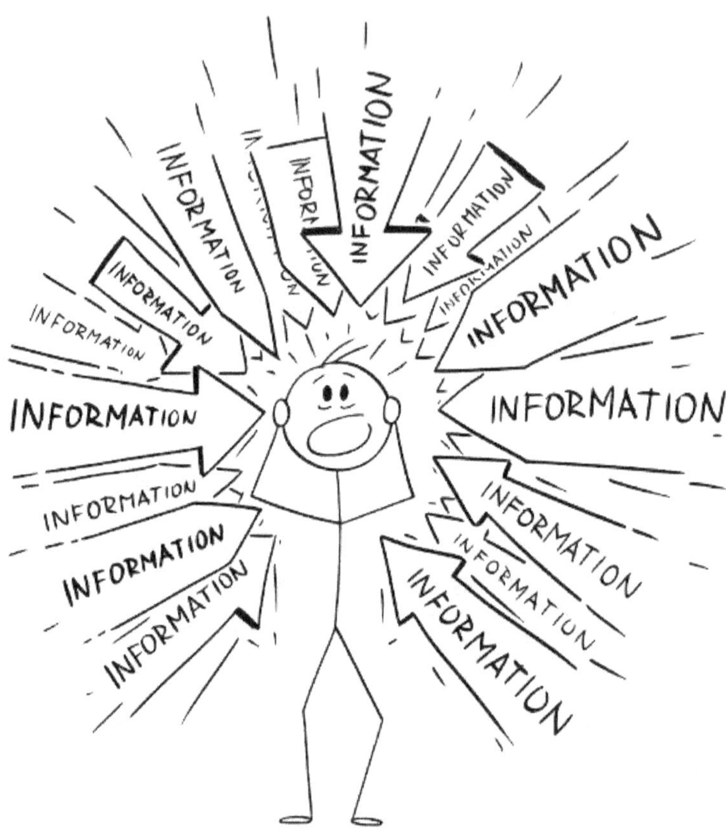

Echo chambers aren't necessarily a bad thing. Simply put, they are environments in the media landscape that reflect and reinforce one's own perceptions and opinions (Wikipedia Contributors, 2019b). Forums on company websites are echo chambers for brands. Communities that form around reality shows, books, Hollywood celebrities, political parties, and games are all examples of echo chambers in the real world.

From Quill to Internet Troll: A Brief Media History

Newspapers are a European invention, the first being handwritten sheets of news that widely circulated on the streets of Venice as early as 1566. These weekly news sheets, or gazettes, conveyed information about political matters and wars in Italy and Europe. Unsurprisingly, gazettes (the granddaddy of newspapers) reached a bigger audience than handwritten news.

The first printed newspaper arose in Germany in 1609. These were heavily censored by governments and could only report on limited topics (chiefly foreign news and current prices). Newspapers continued to enjoy a stymied existence until 1695, when the English government relaxed censorship laws, allowing printed news to flourish in London, Boston, and Philadelphia.

The British colonies located on the eastern coast of the North American continent underwent vast changes between 1675 and 1700 (Kelly, 2016), so understandably, the need for accessible information drove the growth of newspapers.

By the 1830s, high-speed presses could print thousands of copies cheaply. In 1830, the first penny press made its way into the market. It was none other than Lynde M. Walter's *Boston Transcript*. Penny press papers were dirt cheap compared to other newspapers and appealed to a wider audience. Ultimately, they helped to further the spread of literacy. By the 1840s, major and minor cities were linked with telegraph networks, and overnight news became a thing (Wikipedia Contributors, 2022).

Since the dawn of gazettes, the news format has undergone some dramatic changes. Eventually, those changes would pave the way for the 24-hour news cycle of our modern world.

American Broadcast History: A Condensed Version

Some of the most recognizable items in our modern society have an Italian connection. If the concepts of pizza, Gucci, Ferrari, and that beloved gelato had not caught on, our society would have looked drastically different. The same can be said for the very idea of radio.

The Italian inventor, Guglielmo Marconi, developed the idea of the wireless telegraph (the first iteration of radio) in the 1890s. His ideas started to bloom when he sent a wireless Morse Code message to a receiver located more than a kilometer away. As he continued to work on his invention, he received the official British patent for the radio. At its core, it was just a wireless telegraph, but it provided the foundation and impetus for our modern media landscape to develop. Other inventors in the United States and Russia had been developing similar technologies, but Marconi's business savvy moves allowed him to gain the first real connections with this device. By the early 1900s, there were four competing wireless systems. It was the first tentative step toward the Information Age.

The radio boom began in 1919 when Marconi's resources were sold to General Electric, which led to the formation of NBC Radio (back then, it was the Radio Corporation of America). A scant decade later, radio entered a golden age, weathering the stock market crash 1929. By the year 1939, the majority of Americans owned a radio (roughly 80%). During the radio boom, universities offered radio-based courses, churches broadcast services, and newspapers created tie-ins with radio. It was an exciting new medium, and everyone wanted a slice of the airwaves.

By the year 1922, it is believed that 576 licensed radio broadcasters were operational. Radio, essentially, was the TikTok or Instagram of the 1920s and 30s.

In the 1950s and 60s, television began to overtake radio as the chief source of revenue for broadcasting networks. By the time the 60s rolled around, networks ceased to create entertainment programs specifically for radio, but this was not the only change. Radio shifted from formal, stiff 15-minute or hourly programs to the "Top 40" format (Wikipedia Contributors, 2021). This was modern radio as we know it.

The Digital Change to Our Media Landscape

The information-sharing landscape was due for another big shift, and change kept speeding up. During the 1960s, the Internet started as a way for researchers to share information. To give you a bit of perspective, the smartphone in your pocket could easily outperform these early, room-sized beasts that used miles of magnetic tape.

The Cold War was an important catalyst for the evolution of the Internet. With the Soviet Union's launch of the Sputnik satellite into space, the United States Defense Department saw the necessity of finding reliable ways to disseminate information, even after a nuclear strike (Online Library Learning Center, n.d.). Eventually, the first incarnation of the Internet, the Advanced Research Projects Agency Network (ARPANET), would take shape. Technology eventually evolved to a point that allowed two computers to "talk" to each other.

Fast forward a few decades to Web3, and shit has gotten crazy with the metaverse, NFTs, and crypto—all of this became possible on that watershed day, January 1st, 1983, when a universal language connected computers on different networks. Transfer Control Protocol/Internetwork Protocol (TCP/IP) was the new standard, enabling those attention-siphoning social media apps and platforms of today to emerge.

From the First Amendment to Choosing Your News

The United States can pride itself on one fact: Throughout history, our press was (and still is) freer than most other countries. This is all thanks to our courts giving critics of society and the government the freedom to disseminate views that are subversive, unpopular, or even hateful (Epps, 2008). The Founding Fathers knew that the right to report news and circulate opinion without governmental censorship was a hallmark of liberty.

Free press ideals were in the American consciousness long before the oppressive William Cosby, governor of the New York colony in the 1730s, got his knickers in a knot. *Cato's Letters*, a collection of essays published between 1720 and 1723, criticized the British political system long before journalists had a crack at the helm. These letters would frequently be quoted in newspapers that circulated in the American colonies. By 1776, Virginia became the first state to formally protect the press, laying the groundwork for the First Amendment.

Media Freedom Creates Whistleblowers

In 1971, a United States military analyst, Daniel Ellsberg, did the unthinkable. He leaked copies of classified information to *The New York Times*. These documents would come to be known as the *Pentagon Papers* and detailed top-secret political and military involvement in Vietnam from 1945 to 1967 (Biography.com Editors, n.d.). More than that, the *Pentagon Papers* implicated the presidential administrations of Truman, Eisenhower, Kennedy, and Johnson in misleading the public about the degree of U.S. involvement in the matter.

The government reacted with a court order to prevent *The New York Times* from publishing additional excerpts from the papers. They argued that the published materials posed a national security risk. Not satisfied with muzzling the *Times*, a few weeks later, the government tried to block the *Washington Post* from publishing the content, but the courts refused. The Supreme Court would go on to rule in favor of the newspapers in the landmark *New York Times Co. vs. United States* case. This paved the way for both the *Times* and the *Washington Post* to publish content from the *Pentagon Papers* without fear of government censorship.

National security feathers were ruffled to the same degree again some years later. I'm certain you'll be quite familiar with this name: Edward Snowden. The former CIA employee leaked classified documents to the media in the United Kingdom, United States, and Germany in 2013 (History.com Editors, 2018). These leaks revealed surveillance programs that started a heated global debate about government spying. Snowden's actions led some to brand him a traitor, while others hailed him as a hero of media freedom.

The media has had a long and often tumultuous relationship with the government. What a pair of wildcats they are! You never know when the media and government will support or swipe at each other. We could consider whistleblowers a vital cog that helps keep this relation-ship in flux. With the rise of social media, whistleblowers have had a much easier time exposing perceived wrongdoings to the world, but the impact seems to be less earth-shattering than in the days before the Internet. Just recall how quickly the hype died around the Facebook Whistleblower, Frances Haugen.

Us vs. Them: Tribalism and Cancel Culture

Cue the modern world, where information silos, tribalism, and echo chambers have become the norm. How far we have journeyed from those first handwritten news sheets in Venice!

The media landscape in the information age has evolved into a continuum. On the one hand, we have blackhole-like information silos. These are closed systems not designed to "talk" to other systems and control the flow of information, chiefly because they have an incentive to maintain the status quo (Chen, 2019). These systems exist in isolation and are not accessible to the general public, and for good reason!

Just imagine the chaos that would ensue if a hospital's patient records could be freely accessed by the general public. These isolated systems help to protect sensitive data but can result in problems such as information duplication, system bottlenecks, and increased difficulty in reaching a shared consensus. When information becomes difficult to access, it can result in faulty decisions based on inaccurate data.

On the other end of the continuum, we have echo chambers. These are virtual environments where one might encounter information that reflects and reinforces a certain perspective (GCF Global, 2019). Just like an echo that constantly repeats itself in a cave, the viewpoints and opinions in echo chambers only present one side of the story—usually the one with which your perspectives align. It feeds into our confirmation bias. Confirmation bias is a tendency that we all have to only process information consistent with our beliefs (Casad, 2016). This is largely unintentional, but as we learned earlier, the power of story ultimately influences behavior.

Creating Tribes Through Algorithms

Lines of code have an impressive impact and power on our modern world. Social media relies on complex algorithms to curate and display content that lines up with our interests.

Content keeps users scrolling, and digital marketers often like to point out that "Money is in the list" (Javanbakht & Arakcheieva, 2020). In other words, the more customized your experience on these platforms, the less time, money, and effort are needed to use social feeds to sell a particular idea or product. Ideally, brand ambassadors will do most of the heavy lifting.

Just think of your social feeds for a moment. The algorithm shows you content based on your interests. There's practically a video, blog, or community for every topic imaginable. Investing in new tech solutions? There's a whole community dedicated to the topic. Want to forge fantasy weapons like a true blacksmith of yore? There are step-by-step tutorials for that. The beautiful thing about algorithms is that they can help to bring together communities of shared interest, but there's one fly in this digital ointment… Tribalism.

Some of us can still remember what life was like before social media came into being. Social media was a nascent medium that allowed us to connect with friends we had not been in touch with for decades. It was an exciting and dynamic platform that quickly evolved from Friendster and Myspace's rudimentary offerings to video and voice calling at a touch.

The heart and soul of any social media platform is its algorithm. We can see this algorithm at work when we follow our interests. If you have an interest in politics or fitness, you may instantly spot more politically-charged ads and fitness-oriented content in your feed.

Having an algorithm determine what you see on your social feed does not sound inherently evil. So why did Facebook whistleblower Frances Haugen kick up such a stink? Because these algorithms hide a dirty secret: They play on the negativity bias.

As discussed in the previous chapter, this bias leads us to pay more attention to insults than compliments. If you react to a news story (let's say it was one about puppy mills), the algorithm registers your interest in the content and adjusts your feed accordingly. As a result, these algorithms can amplify a negative message and make it easy to spread. After all, spreading a message is a simple "share" or "like" away.

In essence, algorithms help to establish echo chambers and can put forward the idea that we are all part of a "digital tribe." The more content we consume, the more we are fed views and ideologies that will help to keep the echo chamber alive, creating a digital tribe. Just think of all those fitness apps, videos, and tutorials that dominate social media networks. Many of them promote the similar core idea of fitness being good while painting people who are unfit in a negative light. At its very core, tribalism places us in an "us versus them" state of mind.

When we combine that same tribalism with peer pressure, negative emotions, and a bad temper, it can lead to the ostracization of those who disagree with you. A study found that Americans aren't shy about giving someone the digital boot. The majority (61%) reported that they have unfriended, unfollowed, or blocked a person on social media due to their political views or posts (Goodwin, 2020). It is cancel culture at its most elementary.

Social media has not only changed the way we communicate as a species, but the way humans think as well. A book is a long read these days, and it is no wonder! All that doomscrolling and swiping has eroded our attention spans to a scant 2.5 seconds spent on an item in our Facebook feeds (Meta, 2016).

Before the age of social media, our exposure to humanity was a lot more "in-person." We'd visit family and friends for face-to-face time instead of relying on Zoom or FaceTime. We'd read newspapers, magazines, and all manner of print media. There was a greater acceptance of people's differences instead of the "cancel" button being pushed whenever we feel hot under the collar.

Reimagining the Attention Economy

Ever had that feeling where it becomes a struggle to process a simple news story? You may be suffering from information overload. We are bombarded by news and opinions on every social avenue (whether it be online or in-person). But information overload is not as innocuous as one might think. There is darkness lurking behind information overload as it reduces our capacity to function effectively. Coffee would be a perfect example here.

For those of us who love the kick of caffeine in the morning, the vast sea of choices can be overwhelming. From cold coffees in a can to the mythical creations of Starbucks' secret menu, there is no shortage of ways in which to ingest caffeine. You'd think all these choices would make it relatively easy to settle on that paper cup of soy, low fat, no sugar, caramel joy.

The opposite is true, though. When the human brain is presented with too many options, a little something called "analysis paralysis" kicks in. Analysis paralysis is the state where we become unable to make any choices, simply because there are too many to choose from! When analysis paralysis persists, it can lead to burnout.

The idea of information overload is not new and has been floating around since the 1970s. Futurist Alvin Toffler prognosticated about the potential of this form of sensory overload and the challenges it would bring (Wigmore, 2019).

The attention economy has a lot to do with information overload. We may recall our teachers and parents telling us to "pay attention," but what exactly does this phrase mean in the modern world? It means your focus is revenue. The advertising industry (and those it supports) is heavily predicated on the idea that our positive associations with a product or service will increase our likelihood of purchasing their products or services.

They aren't wrong, but it is not the entire story. People make choices for unfathomable reasons sometimes. With all the ads and more coffee choices popping up, the very fabric of the attention economy may be coming undone. At least this is what a report from Midia points out. The report found that consumers do not have the free time to direct their attention to new things (Severin, 2019).

With a million different things screaming for our attention daily, is it only natural that we'd start to prioritize between the attention scream-ers. The report states that competition in the attention economy is more intense than it has ever been. Adding to that, we need to keep in mind that attention is a limited resource; it does not scale.

Just ask yourself, when was the last time you enjoyed a video without the creator trying to sell you a subscription to Skillshare?

Doing Things Differently

Since 2011, the online video game Fortnite has occupied a substantial portion of the attention economy. This seemingly-ubiquitous gaming platform is highly-favored among Gen-Z; its publisher Epic Games has managed to rake in billions through microtransactions and clever advertising. Online games have become a shared culture punctuated with all the nuances of the real world. Cancel culture, trolling, and negativity bias are alive and flourishing in these online domains, yet Fortnite has still managed to hold on to its share of the attention economy.

A change was needed in how content was advertised to younger audiences. Fortnite became a place to hang out with your friends instead of another ad-riddled social platform. Fortnite's approach to treating its platform like a hangout spot was so successful that Netflix mentioned they lose more revenue to Fortnite than HBO (Patches, 2019). The fact that Netflix acknowledges Fortnite as a competitor is significant and points to changing times in the delivery and consumption of stories that matter.

What sets the Fortnite model apart from its competitors in the attention economy is the way changes are implemented. Now and then, Epic rolls out massive updates that overhaul the map and refresh features. They are called "seasons" and serve one purpose: To bring players back for just a little bit longer.

Keep in mind that two to three decades ago, people defined themselves by the music they listened to or the clothes they wore. Today, personal image is as much a part of the virtual world (i.e., how one's Fortnite avatar is dressed) as it is of the physical (Stephen, 2019).

The Power of Memes

People are exhausted by the daily barrage of content. In this sea of information, it becomes increasingly easy to pass along information as the truth, even if that information is patently false. The results can be catastrophic.

Once rumors and stories move from the fringe into mainstream thinking, it can take mere weeks for violence to ensue. This seems to have been the case when a single tweet made a false allegation that liberal philanthropist George Soros was funding Honduran refugees heading to America (Woods & Hahner, 2018). The tweet quickly combined with far-right memes and is believed to have helped motivate an alleged mail-bomber and a mass shooter at a Pittsburgh synagogue.

Memes are effective vehicles of persuasion, fully grabbing hold of those two seconds worth of attention that we are willing to spare. Memes are effective because they get the message across quickly, are highly shareable, and invite people to add their own creative flair (just think of all those *Game of Thrones* memes). Memes don't need to be factual or funny to serve their purpose. All they need to do is attract attention.

Reflect quickly on how often you stop scrolling to enjoy or share a meme. They are effective and highly visual, making them perfect for rapidly distributing information—even if that information is false. Memes are oftentimes stealthy political messages or offer rebellious humor, increasing their shareability. Some memes have become so successful that they are used creatively in advertisements.

Memes are memorable and spread quickly, making them ideal tools for marketers (Bury, 2016). Memes noticed by marketers usually have a humorous element. It makes sense. We remember and associate positive things with those that make us smile.

As much as memes are the perfect advertising tool, these bold, punchy messages can be used to spread false information. Before social media evolved into what it is currently, certain nuggets of information were pretty hard to find. If you wanted to find out more about right-wing extremists, it would be more difficult in the social media dark ages in the early 2010s. In those days, it would be more apt to gather locally or in discreet online forums. Today, information is only a click away, but that does not guarantee the truthfulness of the content you find.

The memes made the alleged Pittsburgh mail bomber's case quite interesting. His van was covered in images and slogans often found on fringe and right-wing social media accounts. That's not where he found those memes, though. He found them in his social feed, an algorithm recommendation based on his previous activity.

Social media platforms have tried to fight the scourge of hate speech and conspiracy theories, but it remains a difficult task. We only need to look at the 2021 United States Capitol attack to see how promoters of fringe ideas find ways to share their thinking on well-trafficked social media, where algorithms do the heavy lifting. Often, these ideas trigger their own echo chambers, drawing more attention to themselves.

So how does this all tie into what you see on your social media feed? Simple. "Noise" is all those items in your feed that you scroll past. Attention is a commodity being pulled in a million directions, which is why a story that matters is more important than ever. When you are ready to learn *how* to tell stories that matter, and earn your customer or target market's attention, then proceed to the next chapter. Be ready to be challenged…and to have a little fun.

3

———

STORIES THAT F*CKING MATTER™

There are three core principles to telling a story that really fucking matters.

The Three Pillars of STFM™

Roots: This is where you came from; it also shapes your perspective and creates a connection with your audience. Where you came from, your family history, education, and experience all help to color the lens through which you view the world and how you tell stories. Whether you were an army brat that lived in different places or went to a public school, these experiences help to connect you with others by providing context and building familiarity.

Stakes: This refers to the level of risk and investment you have undertaken and sacrificed in your life or career. *Stakes* keep people engaged and interested in you and your story, and creates drama and intensity. *Stakes* give your audience a reason to continue paying attention to your brand. They show your commitment and why you (and they) should care, building trust along the way.

Impact:

This is your idea or solution. Your *Impact* helps with enrolling others in your vision. Put yourself in your customer's shoes. What *Impact* does your solution create? Your answer needs to highlight the benefits your audience can gain. It could be a book that helps people learn why meditation is important. It could be an initiative benefiting cancer patients. Define your target audience clearly, e.g., single mothers, first-time crypto buyers, etc.

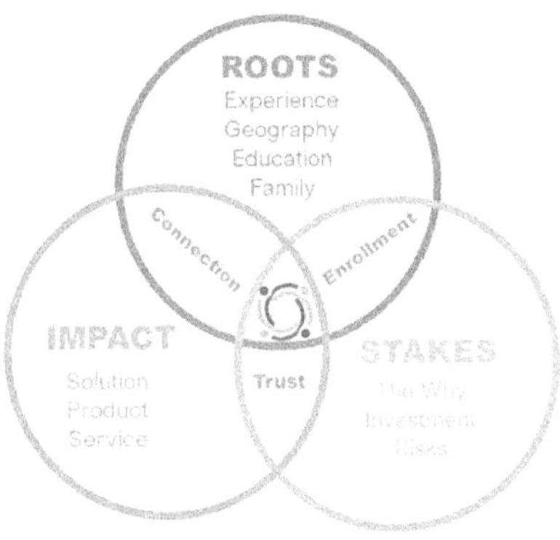

The Stories That F*cking Matter™ Model

When these three pillars are woven together, you create a story that fucking matters, cuts through the clutter and gets noticed! We'll discuss each of these three pillars more in-depth in the chapters that follow.

When The Stars Align

The secret to an impactful story is patience and knowing your audience. This certainly was the case when my dear friend Danny Pintauro decided it was time to share his own truth with the world.

Danny was a popular child actor during the 80s and 90s and one of the first major celebrities to courageously come out publicly—within just weeks of Ellen DeGeneres' coming out. Danny was known for starring on the long-running ABC TV sitcom *Who's The Boss* alongside Judith Light, Tony Danza, and Alyssa Milano.

As a young gay kid growing up in New Jersey, where Danny is originally from, I looked up to him. He was someone that I, Steven, could relate to, and I admired him even more for coming out after the show ended. When I moved to L.A., Danny and I ended up meeting and becoming fast friends. In one of our early get-togethers, he confided in me a personal story he wanted to share with the world. It was a story that he felt was educational and significant, and one that he had been holding onto for years. The only member of the media who he knew could do his story justice was Oprah Winfrey.

As a publicist, I had my work cut out for me. Oprah doesn't just interview anybody! But I knew it was worthy of her attention. I reached out to Oprah's people only to learn disappointing news. Her show was coming to an end! They had a few more episodes left in the last season but had already finished filming. That was in 2011. Perhaps it was a sign that the world wasn't quite ready for Danny's story just yet. So, Danny held in his story for another four years.

In 2015, Oprah's producers reached back out to inquire if Danny was ready to tell his story. After we spoke on the phone, one of her producers told me she would run the idea by Oprah within the hour and get back to me. I didn't put much faith in that, but an hour later, I got a reply. Oprah would love to have Danny on her show, *Where Are They Now?* What incredible news!

After preparing and coaching Danny for his appearance over the next couple of weeks, his entire team joined him at the OWN production studio in Los Angeles while he shot the interview with Oprah. It was exciting and nerve-wracking. Until the episode aired, we were basically sworn to silence for the next six months. Meanwhile, Grapevine's and Oprah's teams worked in tandem to make sure we were maximizing this immense opportunity. In September 2015, the story broke and became the number one trending news story. Twitter, Yahoo, and headlines everywhere revealed Danny's truth about his HIV status and past struggles with crystal meth addiction. Being silent for all those months was worth it.

We rolled out a major campaign to keep attention on this impactful and personal issue in the news cycle. ABC's *The View* picked up the story and invited Danny to New York for an interview with fellow former child stars Raven Symone and Candace Cameron Bure.

Although Bure attempted to grill and perhaps even shame him, Danny continued with his mission to articulate his personal story to viewers and address the stigma around HIV status by confronting and dispelling many dangerous myths surrounding the subject. At one point, in a completely unprecedented moment, Bure put Danny's husband Wil Pintauro-Tabares on the spot in the audience by asking him on-camera if the married couple uses condoms. I stood in the area behind the set with my mouth on the floor watching the studio monitors. I was disgusted, appalled, shocked, and disappointed with Bure. How tasteless and tactless.

When Danny was asked by Bure why he felt he was the best person to be a role model, he eloquently responded with, "I don't want to be a hero. I don't want to be the role model. I want to be the example of what can happen if you get into drugs, if you're being promiscuous, if you're not taking care of yourself, if you're not being checked, if you're not living a healthy, responsible lifestyle."

By rebranding himself as a cautionary tale, Danny took overwhelmingly negative events and turned them into something positive. There was a bit of backlash from HIV advocacy groups and other individuals nationwide, though. The language used during the interview was identified as problematic and filled with stigma (Kruger, 2015). Danny knew his story was a much-needed wake-up call for those who spouted junk science and moralism as HIV prevention tools, which made his story resonate all the more.

Steven and Danny Backstage at The View, 2015

Steven and Danny on the Beacon of Light Press Tour, 2015

Why Danny's Story Fucking Mattered

America has always loved a good redemption story.

As a returning prodigal son, Danny did not deliver his story as a dry, public service announcement. He was unafraid to be real, vulnerable, and raw. The risks were high! After all, our society still treats HIV status as some lurid game of peekaboo and associates a positive status with questionable behavior. When his story broke, Danny risked more than the wrath of cancel culture. He risked his entire way of life, yet his story was demanding to be told.

Naturally, Danny's story was a big deal for me (and Grapevine PR). We successfully secured Danny an exclusive sit-down interview with Oprah Winfrey. So many outlets wanted to share a version of Danny's story. Danny embarked on an international educational media tour, which he called *The Beacon of Light Tour*. It was the perfect example of a story that fucking mattered and reminded me why I got into PR in the first place.

A good story is not always about selling something. It is about changing people's hearts and minds. Danny's story did exactly that.

He ended up becoming a celebrity ambassador for the Elizabeth Taylor AIDS Foundation, earning a number of accolades for his courage and advocacy. We won countless awards, as well, for Media Campaign of the Year and PR Agency of the Year.

It was a magical ride, a career highlight, and a significant achievement for Grapevine. Most importantly, it was a PR highlight for Danny, who waited patiently to have his story told the right way.

Something amazing happened when Danny's story broke: It reignited a very important public conversation about HIV/AIDS. His bravery encouraged other celebrities to break their silence. Charlie Sheen revealed his HIV-positive status in an interview on the *Today Show*. Billy Porter, Jonathan Van Ness, and other celebrities have also since revealed their statuses in the media cycle, helping to keep the conversation alive and relevant.

Learning from Expert Storytellers

Stories that matter can sometimes be inspired by unusual events. Ryan Breslow, the founder of the fintech startup Bolt, certainly knew how to dominate headlines with something that mattered: implementing a permanent four-day work week.

The decision was not made lightly. The company conducted a three-month trial. During this trial phase, certain employees would have a four-day work week. The response to the trial was overwhelmingly positive, leading to the four-day work week becoming permanent. The media loved it, and Breslow maximized the *Impact*. He used the opportunities to share the values of his company (thinking like a founder). Giving his target audience something positive to associate with the company was brilliant.

"We're minimizing the amount of time you have to be in meetings. With the time you now have, if you think like a founder, you might want to go to a conference. You might want to work on your personal development. You might want to spend time with your family," Breslow said on the topic of company culture (Mehta, 2022).

Take a closer look at the quote now. Did you notice how effortlessly Breslow crafted a story that mattered? It ticks all the boxes. It is short, and even a child can understand it. He lets you know exactly why the four-day work week matters, a strategy that worked brilliantly to break through today's fragmented and frenzied media landscape.

Keep in mind that at the time, the media landscape was covering the Great Resignation from all angles, making Bolt's adoption of a four-day work week a perfect story to highlight. It is a little thing that we call "trendjacking."

"Trendjacking," or "news-jacking," is a technique that can help to introduce your solution to a larger audience. By capitalizing on the newsworthiness of a current topic being heavily covered in the news cycle, your solution can be introduced to a much larger and more substantial audience (Le Vine, 2022b). It is a potent technique that worked beautifully in Bolt's favor, but like all good things, there's plenty of room for mishaps if implemented incorrectly.

There are so many people in the world who have stories worth telling, but they don't know how to tell them. Their stories, as impactful and compelling as they may be, remain untold. Their voices were silenced. This does not have to be you once you know how to tell a *Story That Fucking Matters*. Some of the most successful people in recent history are storytellers who have mastered the three elements of a compelling story–*Roots*, *Stakes*, and *Impact*, which we will cover next.

Richard Branson

Branson was not one to shy away from freely sharing what he thinks, sees, and does. These values are expressed in the Virgin brand. He cleverly makes use of nuance and tells his stories, flaws and all. Branson's success speaks volumes as to why we should tell our own stories, flaws and all.

Branson's story clearly pulls from all three key pillars of an STFM. Born in 1950s England, Branson learned how not only to cope with ADHD and dyslexia but to persevere despite the challenges they posed. He grew up in a family that didn't have much money. And at 16, he dropped out of boarding school.

But that was just the beginning of his story, not the end. He founded *Student*, a free magazine in which he was able to circulate 50,000 copies. And just a few years later, he founded Virgin Records, becoming one of the top record labels in the world. Since then, he has launched an airline, a telecom company, a space tourism company, hotels, cruise lines, and much more.

Branson has an epic story, highlighting every one of the pillars of an STFM brilliantly. His *Roots*: His childhood in England with a family that struggled to make ends meet. His *Stakes*: Not allowing his ADHD and dyslexia to hinder his ability to succeed in school and in business —and becoming an entrepreneur at a young age after dropping out of school. His *Impact*: His businesses and philanthropic ventures.

Bruce Springsteen

Great storytelling creates a shared experience. "The Boss" gave us decades of the American experience through songs. He often draws inspiration from other people for his music.

Springsteen is one of my favorite examples of the power of an STFM. From a personal standpoint, I have always connected with him. We grew up in the same small, blue-collar town in New Jersey and attended the same high school (at different times, of course). The "hometown" he sings of is my own, Freehold Borough—and he was a close friend of my family.

His brand *is* his story. His songs have pulled from his *Roots*, *Stakes*, and *Impact* since day one of his songwriting career – and have been a major part of his massive appeal. His lyrics bear witness to many of the same experiences those growing up in America in the latter half of the 20th century have also experienced. Because of this, his fans have been able to form a unique connection with him, feeling a sense of familiarity and camaraderie with him.

Steve Jobs

The man who based an entire career on stories has to be included on any list of storytellers. You know you are a great storyteller when others are repeating your story. By creating an experience worth sharing, Jobs got others to tell his story. These stories were memorable, resonated with the target audience, and were backed up by facts.

His own story is one for the ages.

Sheryl Sandberg

Sandberg, formerly the Chief Operation Officer of Facebook (now Meta Platforms, Inc) is not afraid to use her position to address problems in society, currently via the non-profit she founded LeanIn.Org. Her stories are relatable, and she taps into personal experiences to generate empathy from her audience. Sandberg shows us that sharing personal stories is highly effective at creating connections between the target audience and a brand.

Tony Robbins

Tony's story is one that too many Americans may be familiar with. Life in a 400-square-foot apartment and less-than-humble beginnings. The inspirational story of how his company got started and his journey through life is a lesson in the power of language.

I'll let you in on a little secret; we all have a story to share. Never assume a story is too ordinary to share. Tony's stories work because they make the audience root for the underdog.

The Common Thread of all Great Storytellers

These great storytellers all have one common element in their stories. They simplify on two levels. First, the story is short. It can "fit on the back of an envelope," in the words of Richard Branson. Secondly, they use easy-to-understand language, even when explaining complicated subjects or ideas. By simplifying a story, it becomes easier to build rapport with your target audience, bringing you a step closer to making headlines.

When done right, storytelling can become an effective marketing tool to grow a business. There's a bit of psychology behind this because stories help us to remember things. Some of the most effective stories don't need an audience to listen actively to get the message across. Storytelling can reach audiences on a personal level. If compelling enough, stories can motivate audiences to engage with your brand on various levels. This engagement will help to build your following, which is why authors, speakers, and coaches try to remain active on social media.

When building a following for your brand, keep in mind that content is king, so try to weave your stories into all your content—this is how you earn good press.

But first thing's first…it's one thing to be able to tell a great story; it's another thing to tell a great story and have it land properly with its intended audience. So, let's talk about that. Who is your audience?

Defining Your Audience: To Whom It Should Fucking Matter

The better we understand our target audience, the more *qualified, relevant* people your brand will be able to reach. Target audiences are those people who are likely to show an interest in your products or services. Your job is to reach them. This is where building audience personas out of common characteristics such as demographics and psychographics can lend us a helping hand.

When you begin to identify your target audience, don't be afraid to get specific (Newberry, 2018). Start with broad categories, like "millennials" or "athletes," and fine-tune it from there. It is best practice to speak directly to your best potential customers, so having a clear understanding of your target audience will help you succeed in this attention economy. The basic concept is rooted in narrowing your focus and expanding your brand's reach in the process.

Gaining a Basic Understanding

Starting with the people already engaged with your brand can lead to valuable insights. Some data points worth considering are:

Age: You don't need to be hyper-specific here, but you need to at least know the age range.

Language: Don't assume your target audience speaks the same language as you do. If you are the owner of a designer shoe brand targeting the *haute couture* crowd in Paris, you need to consider how cultural and language differences will impact your storytelling approach.

Spending Patterns: Is your target audience working class or globe-trotting executives? Knowing your target audience's level of discretionary income or spending power is a crucial nugget of information that can't be overlooked.

Interests: Here is where we focus on trying to identify with whom or what our target audience interacts. The goal is to gain an understanding of their interests. This information can help us frame our story in a relatable way.

Challenges: These are the pain points with which your target audience is contending and the problems your product or service intends to solve.

Stage of Life: College students, new parents, and retirees are all at different stages in their lives. Their stage of life will dictate the solutions that appeal to them and the language they use. If you are going to use slang in your story, keep in mind it should be age-appropriate. Otherwise, the impact will be lost. Slang that appeals to one age group might be completely misunderstood or offensive to another age group.

Fine-tuning Your Audience

Much of this information can be gleaned from social media analytics. When you dive into your existing customer database, UTM codes—snippets of code attached to the end of a URL used to measure the effectiveness of digital marketing campaigns—become indispensable tools to gather information about who clicks on your content (Newberry, 2019).

Social listening is a great way to uncover conversations about your brand. By monitoring relevant hashtags and keywords, you'll be able to discover what people are saying about your brand. The key is using relevant keywords, though. Reaching out and responding to posts on various platforms is a great way to find and fine-tune your target audience. Remember, your efforts will only be effective if you can reach your audience on the social channels they are using! If your target audience is mostly on Facebook, it won't make sense to attempt to reach them through Reddit or TikTok. This is where UTM codes come in handy too, as they reveal where your referral traffic is coming from.

Don't hesitate to check out your competition. Chances are your target market may overlap with that of your competition, so it's worth checking them out. You might benefit from lessons they have already learned, which can be a great time saver. Take a look at who they are targeting and how they reach their audiences.

Having a rock-solid understanding of how your brand makes your audience's lives better, easier, or more interesting will help you get the right message across. IKEA makes use of this strategy quite successfully. The advertised furniture may be small, functional, or inexpensive, but it doesn't fail to communicate the message of convenience and comfort. Think about how your brand can create value for its audience, but keep these three points in mind:

1. Your audience's purchasing barriers and possible ways to overcome them.
2. Where they are on their purchasing journey. Are they in research mode, combing through reviews, or ready to buy?
3. The kind of content your audience interacts with.

The basic principles of defining a target audience go back to the early days of marketing. In 1979, fashion retailer, The Limited, defined its target audience as this: 16- to 35-year-old females that are educated, affluent, and fashion-oriented, who work and live in major metropolitan areas (Walters & White, 1987). Patagonia also has a very clear target audience in mind: Consumers between the ages of 18 and 35 who are conscious about what they buy, enjoy nature and the outdoors, and maintain an active lifestyle.

Keep Your Audience in Mind

When weaving your story, your audience should be at the forefront of consideration. Some stories make us laugh. Some make us cry. Not all stories will evoke the same response from everyone. When you browse through your bank of stories, consider what your audience cares about, their values, goals, and interests.

When I address female audiences, I tend to get more personal and raw, but when I address buttoned-up businessmen, my stories are flavored with the quest for empathy. When addressing an Eastern audience, your story structure will change a little. For example, Americans love to hear stories where the protagonist overcomes hardships. It is a value we hold in our pursuit of the American Dream. In the East, stories are more often used as cautionary tales where one learns from the protagonist's mistakes.

Ask yourself why you are qualified to be the audience's guide. A fitness professional might tell stories about when they first began their fitness journey and the roadblocks they encountered and overcame. It takes a lot of courage to share these little nuggets of your soul, but your audience will relate easier because of it. Telling a personal story is the most powerful form of communication humans possess (Duarte, 2018). However, these stories need to be told from a place of conviction.

4

———

ROOTS: THE ORIGIN STORY TO BUILD CONNECTION

Have you ever considered what spurs the creativity and passion you've poured into your ideas? The answer to this question is important. It forms the first pillar of a story that fucking matters. For many, the answer lies in their past.

Our *Roots*, the background from which we come, informs the way we see the world and how others perceive us. For better or worse, our family background, education, job experience, volunteerism, or neighborhood where we grew up informs and molds our perspective. The beautiful thing is that everyone will have a unique perspective to introduce to their audiences. By sharing what makes you tick, your audience can connect and relate to you powerfully.

I saw the most interesting sign in my friend's dance studio. It read: "If you enter the studio, do so with passion!" My friend studied classical ballet from the age of five and wanted to pursue it as a career. For him, the ultimate goal was the stage. According to him, ballet dancers have an obligation the moment they set foot on the stage to make the audience feel something. And this is quite applicable to the world of business too.

When your solution takes center stage, it is your duty and mission to help your audience connect. That's where the background comes in. Everyone's past affects what they do today.

Think about all the things you do with vigor and the experiences you've had in your lifetime. How does your background affect what you do? These are the kinds of stories to share with your audience.

Telling Your Origin Story

In our world of increasing choices and distractions, a story may be the one thing that saves you from being lost in the sea of content.

People, it turns out, are hardwired for stories. Researcher and author Kendall Haven summarized the results of a lengthy study on persuasiveness and memory (Ritchie, 2017). He investigated the different kinds of story structures that would make a persuasive attempt more memorable and successful. Through anecdotes and trials, it was discovered that people respond best to stories that follow a general structure.

- *The character should have a goal backed by a clear, understandable motive.*
- *Every good origin story will point out the obstacles and consequences of failure the character has had to face and overcome.*
- *Once the obstacles are overcome, the goal is reached, and everything stands still until a new event stirs things up.*

For a lot of us, this sounds like the basic makings of every comic book, novel, movie, and game on the planet. The basic story recipe is every-where because it works so well!

In a world where we are saturated with choice, your story may be the deciding factor between success and failure. Think about that for a moment.

If you are the founder of a company, your target audience will likely want to know what problems you sought to solve and how you've worked to do so (Alviani, 2018). They'll want to know the origin story of the business. That story will determine a brand's persona and what community will resonate with your story. So, origin stories are pretty damn important.

Origin stories typically include details like why and how a company got started, who started it, and where. It is the backbone on which all your brand's future stories will be based. An origin story is not that short bio on your "about" page, nor is it an opportunity for the vain to tell the world how wonderful they are.

No, an origin story is how your brand came to be. It helps to introduce your brand and frame your motivations in a way that elicits connection. At least, that is the ideal we strive for.

The most basic origin story will give your audience a sense of who you are. Should the story prove to be convincing enough, it can become a determining factor in people's choices to purchase, invest in, or work for your brand. When you are competing for business, investor funding, and talent, stories make a difference because they are unique (or at least they're supposed to be).

No one has your experience or unique perspective, so your story can lure people or send them into a deep sleep of forgetfulness.

An origin story alone does not guarantee success or a fanatical following. Many people may feel unequipped for the task of writing their brand's origin story. Whatever creative process you choose, it is important to remember that a story should be driven by its founder. Your vision and the word magic of a good copywriter are vital ingredients to the beginnings of a good origin story that matters.

The only thing worse than having no origin story is a boring one. Carefully reflect on what you would like to include in your brand's origin story. Here are a few pointers that will help you critique and write a noteworthy origin story.

Be honest, and don't act like you have it all figured out. Be open about the fact that you had no clue what you were doing when you started. Even serial entrepreneurs have stared cluelessly at their business plans at some point.

Don't be afraid to talk about your failures, but don't dwell on them. The idea is to let your target audience know your path was not a bed of roses, but you prevailed, nonetheless.

Write in the first person. Talking about yourself or your brand in the third person just sounds awkward. Unless you are a seasoned journalist, leave this style of reporting to the newspapers.

Keep it to the point. This does not mean you need to have a short origin story (but it does not mean you have to retell *The Odyssey* either). Find the golden middle where you provide just enough detail to help people relate to and understand your journey.

Make it saucy! Remember the origin story of *Squirrel Girl*? It is a Marvel comic created by Will Murray and Steve Ditko, and her origin goes something like this: She was born and grew a tail. Yep. That's inspiring superhero origins for you. You'd think the same franchise that was responsible for Thanos and Doctor Doom would have fleshed out the origin stories of their comic book characters beyond forgettable tedium, but surprisingly, a large number of comic book characters have forgettable backstories. The same can be said for many brands out there!

Where you publish your origin story is up to you. It can take the shape of a blog post, video, podcast, or even a mini-documentary on your business website. Just make sure the format you use will work well for the audience you are trying to reach. If you need examples of good origin stories, just take a look at Slack's journey from a whimsical online game to a software giant. Harley-Davidson's origin paints a touching picture of how the founders figured out how to fit engines onto bicycle frames—all in a small shed in Milwaukee in the early 1900s.

Your origin story does not have to be an epic tale. Just remember to keep it simple, straightforward, and authentic. The purpose of the origin story is to welcome people onto your journey, giving them a frame of reference for the founder, brand, and the values they hold dear.

Improving Connection Through Authentic Brand Storytelling

More brands are learning to appreciate the power a good story has to transform their online presence and more importantly, to build a connection with their target audience. Iconic brands like Coca-Cola and Disney have long used the power of narrative to connect with their audiences, while companies like Apple have leveraged storytelling to legendary status.

Stories have an interesting impact on the human brain, and researchers have found that our brain responds to the descriptive power of stories so deeply that the sensory and motor cortex can be influenced (Paul, 2012). If a storyteller is talking about kicking a ball, the motor part of the listener's brain that would kick a ball in real life actually lights up!

Remember Nightbirde's tear-jerking audition on *America's Got Talent*? That's the power of story. Her origin story had it all: her reason for being on the show, her struggle, and the resolution (her calm acceptance of her fate). Her story and the way she told it (in song format) resonated with audiences. For a fleeting second, you could experience the world through her eyes and connect with her perspective. The scientific community calls this shared experience "neural coupling" (NarrativeIQ, n.d.).

A narrative approach makes your story more memorable. When we listen to a story, our language processing areas and other areas in the brain are activated. Events in the story you are telling could trigger certain parts of the brain to activate in your listener.

Typically, several neural pathways are activated when we listen to or tell a memorable story, and the increased brain activity helps us retain information better. Work done by Dr. Uri Hasson, Ph.D., at Princeton University, has illustrated the power that story has on neural coupling. The short definition of neural coupling is a state where our minds almost "synchronize" in a way. Similar areas in the brain would become active in both the storyteller and the listener.

Successful neural coupling results in building connections and trust (Stephens et al., 2010). By telling an authentic origin story, you can connect and build trust with your audience on a biological level. This work has tremendous implications for how business is conducted today.

Regardless of your business size or type, you'll need stories to drive your brand's growth. Once a founder understands the power that stories hold—the power to communicate, influence, engage, and inspire—you'll find that stories have become a core part of their business methodology (Patel, 2019).

So, we know that sharing your *Roots* can help build connection and rapport with others and that your original story should follow a basic blueprint. Does that mean any stories about your background will generate the effects you desire? No. Your story still needs other elements to be effective.

Other Elements That Comprise Compelling Origin Stories

There's more to creating a convincing origin story than finding a likely narrative and bastardizing it with marketing materials. Your brand story will need:

> *Personality*: Brand stories are often treated as marketing materials, ads, or sales pitches. This is a grave mistake, as brand stories need to be told with the writer's (or founder's) personality in the foreground. Make no mistake, this is not the time for founders to adopt a god-like persona that infuses a company with life.

Instead, skew your story to be inspired by people. Develop a saga of continual growth. Dull stories won't attract or retain an audience. Just reflect on how Red Bull paints its brand's personality: Lively, energetic, and daring. It is a persona that suits the brand and is reflected in the way it uses language to talk to its audience and to describe itself. Reflecting on your brand's persona and the impression you want your audience to have is a key ingredient to creating a story that matters. You'll know you've nailed your brand's origin story when the ending feels like the start of an exciting new adventure.

Focus: This is where many entrepreneurs miss the bus! The focus of your story will answer one crucial question: "Why does your brand exist?"

Just a quick heads up, "making money" is not the limp answer your audience is looking for. Your answer needs substance to flesh out the reason why your brand came into being. Your answer requires you to tell a story, and your goal should be to answer the question, "Why should I buy from you?"

A Connection With Your Audience: Origin stories should be relatable to your target audience. If your target audience is active and adventure-minded it will do you no good to use stories and language to convey a lackadaisical image. Remember, your story communicates the ideals associated with your brand.

Let's take the author of a book titled *Crypto for Everyone*. The title of this fictional work would imply that crypto has been simplified for everyone to understand. What story do you think will resonate best with the reader? One where the author starts as a crypto-millionaire, or one where the author shares the journey to becoming a crypto-millionaire? Quite frankly, most people don't have financially carefree starts to their lives, so beginning the narrative as a millionaire may create a disconnect. An author has a better chance of connecting with their audience if *the journey* to that colossal bank account was shared instead.

Always reflect on the message you want your brand to convey and compare it to the message your brand is currently sending out. Chances are you'll discover a disconnect somewhere.

Get Others to Tell Your Story: A good story is easy to share. There are a few things you can do to increase the shareability of your brand's story. Infusing your brand with personality, being active on social media, and encouraging your customers to spread the word are all sound tactics to get you that needed exposure. Actively communicate using a story format.

Whether you are writing a guest post, a biography, or revamping the "about" section on your website, harness the power of storytelling to get your point across. Entrench your brand's narrative in all your business activities. That way, when your brand becomes a mainstream sensation, your origin story will become further entrenched in public awareness. After all, you've laid the groundwork for it to happen!

Avoiding Conclusion Confusion

Have you ever experienced a story where the conclusion was disappointing and anticlimactic? It does not matter if it is a news article, interview, song, book, film, or series. A confusing conclusion is a sure-fire way to suck the life out of a great story.

The Handmaid's Tale is a great example of conclusion confusion. After doing a brilliant job of setting up the story and guiding the reader throughout the tale, the author ended the book in a manner that left some readers with more lingering questions. Whether by accident or design, questions about the character Offred and those people who took the protagonist away will live rent-free in readers' heads. For some, this can completely detract from the experience and ruin a good story.

A story provides the framework for a business to become a brand. The story should not strive to trap the audience, but it should be a catalyst to spark interest. Sometimes we get so caught up in the story that we forget the conclusion matters. It is fine to honor your brand's heritage and your *Roots*, but don't get trapped in the past. Your story should live in the present and be rooted in your brand's values. The conclusion should therefore point to where the brand is heading without generating additional questions.

Ask yourself, what is your brand's origin story and what impression do you want to leave your audience with?

5

STAKES: LEVEL OF RISK, INVESTMENT, OR SACRIFICE

The Definition of "Stakes"

Every story needs drama to keep the plot moving and the audience engaged. That is where the *Stakes* come in.

Stakes center around the entrepreneur, the level of risks, and investment of time, resources, and passion. A story without *Stakes* may feel flat and will not hold your audience's attention. So, what exactly do I mean by *Stakes*?

Let's say the founder of an organic baby food venture wants to identify their story using the three pillars of an STFM (*Roots, Stakes,* and *Impact*). That founder will first need to take inventory of where they grew up, their family, educational background, work and volunteer experience, etc.

By sharing their perspective, the founder can build context and familiarity with their audience. Maybe they grew up in poverty with a single mother who had to drop out of high school and work three jobs. Perhaps they worked several part-time jobs to put themselves through college. Remember, the *Roots* of a story are all about creating context and helping your audience to "see" through your eyes.

When the founder of our fictional organic baby food company has their *Roots* pinned down, that's when the drama comes in. We want our audience to understand why we took the risk.

Continuing with this example, the founder invested all their life savings into their idea and worked on it as a side job to their day job. It adds some spice to our story arc and lets us know the level of commitment.

Stakes have three defining characteristics: Risk, investment, and passion. I'll explain each characteristic in turn.

Risks: Business requires a healthy amount of risk and sacrifice.

If you play your cards right, the risks you are taking can make for a wonderful origin story! Whether you left a stable day job to start your own venture or created a business as a single parent, there was some amount of risk and sacrifice along the way. Maybe it was the loss of a stable income, or perhaps you had to sacrifice time with your children. Perhaps you risked it all and went from living out of a camper van to being a successful business tycoon. As in the world of investment, your risk tolerance will determine how big a leap you'd be willing to take.

Investment: Money is a replaceable investment.

The investment we are referring to is not something that can be printed by the Treasury Department. We are talking about time and resources. You poured your blood, sweat, and tears into seeing your vision come to life. Maybe you took out a home equity line of credit to fund your startup. Maybe you used your home as collateral. Maybe the business evolved from a side hustle into a multimillion-dollar brand. Perhaps you have got investors or invested your life savings into your business concept. Whatever shape it takes, time and resources (whether they be material things or expert knowledge) have been poured into the realization of your vision.

Passion: The world would be dead if not for passion!

Passion is the drive that compelled you to start your business in the first place. It is the "why" in the story of your business that will help them answer the question: "Why should I support your business?"

Nobody wants their solution to be branded as a gimmick. That's why the *Stakes* are so important. Apart from creating drama in the story arc, it shows our audience just how invested we are in the pursuit of our vision and our ideas.

When reflecting on your vision, think of the risks you have taken and the sacrifices you have endured to make it happen. Those stories build credibility with your audience. Think of credibility as a judgment call that our audiences make based on how believable our storytelling is (O'Quinn, 2016). You wouldn't purchase products or services from a brand that you did not deem credible, so don't expect anything different from your audience.

My Story

Some people just have their lives figured out and planned down to the last detail. I didn't, but I knew one truth about myself: I was a born storyteller.

All throughout high school, my dad would take me to used CD shops and record shows, where I started collecting memorabilia such as back-stage passes, posters, and bootlegs of concerts of all my favorite musical artists. The evidence was plastered all over my room. Music was my life. I'd hand out copies of albums I loved to my classmates, telling them how much they needed to listen to them. It was only later in life that I realized it was the stories behind the music and the artists that drove and motivated me.

Their powerful lyrics enriched my life, moved me, and ultimately led me to find my own identity.

I've always been a storyteller, sharing stories about places I've been or crazy and funny experiences. In fact, in college, my Creative English professor, Mr. Ridley, upon reading my journal, stated bluntly in front of the class, "Steven Le Vine, I wish I could live in your brain for just one day!"

Teenage Steven in High School Courtyard, 1999

Teenage Steven wearing a Lisa Loeb tee on a family cruise in 1998

My father was a human resources expert who prided himself on matching people's personalities with careers. He spotted my love for promoting musicians a long time ago. On his advice, I went on to study public relations and communications. I was hooked!

Throughout college, I made a point of joining all sorts of public relations groups and co-founded some as well. I ended up doing some PR for those same organizations and writing music reviews for my university's newspaper and the now defunct online music magazine, *Kitty Magik*.

After graduating from college, I started working as an intern at a top New Jersey PR, marketing and events agency, Allen Consulting. Its founder, Sylvia Allen, was a family friend and quickly became a mentor to me. With Allen at the helm, her agency has had an impeccable track record for more than four decades and has taken home dozens of awards.

I eased into my new role focusing on local events and nonprofits with the knowledge that I wanted to eventually create something of my own as well. But this vision wasn't years in the making. It was days. In fact, only a couple of them.

A week into my internship, I began representing a musician on the side. It was a hobby. I wasn't giving the story behind my company much thought—yet. I created a logo and a company name (grapeVine Promotions) for formality, but it was still only a side project in my mind. And it quickly got put on hold when the opportunity to work at a corporate PR firm focusing on real estate arose only a few months later.

As an assistant account executive, I was basically a paid intern who happened to be getting clients press in the *Wall Street Journal*—a feat I was told only the vice presidents at the firm could pull off. While the experience was great, the corporate PR world was not something I wanted to do. I knew I was not being true to my *Roots*. I wanted to tell the stories of those in music and entertainment.

Lesson in Patience

More than 25 years ago, Harold Abramson thought he saw a real-estate play in the Catskill Mountains, just north of New York City. The area, which had once been a popular retreat for city dwellers had fallen on hard times. However, rumors abounded that nearby Stewart Air Force Base in Newburgh, N.Y., would become a large commercial airport and that the Catskills would open their doors to legalized gambling.

So Mr. Abramson decided to buy apartments in Middletown, N.Y., and cash in on the coming boom. Mr. Abramson's company, Value Group, bought a 276-unit complex that had been foreclosed on, but were unable to secure an adjacent 11 acres. It hardly mattered. The promised good times never came. No gambling. No big airport.

Now, after all these years—long after Harold Abramson had died and his son, Andrew, is running the company—Value Cos., which became the company's name last year, finally acquired the acreage for $1.7 million in December. (The sellers, **Power Realty** LLC of New York, didn't return calls seeking comment.) Meanwhile, the Port Authority of New York and New Jersey is moving forward with plans to purchase Stewart International Airport, which handled about 300,000 passengers last year, and convert it into one that would handle 1.3 million annually. And just this month, New York Gov. Eliot Spitzer announced an agreement with the St. Regis Mohawk Tribe for a casino at Monticello Raceway, though hurdles still exist. "In our minds, it wasn't a question of whether but of when," said Jon Moore, vice president of development for Value Cos.

A client press placement secured by Steven in the Wall Street Journal

Grapevine PR was revived. This time, I decided to focus on what I loved doing most: Helping others tell their stories.

My PR firm would center around entertainment. I made a bold move and reached out to actor, magician, and improv artist Michael Carbonaro. The same Michael from truTV's *The Carbonaro Effect*. He had been in some independent comedies and on TV at the time. I wrote to him on MySpace, introducing myself and my company. That spring of 2007, he became a client.

Soon after, I began meeting with others, including Anthony Rapp, an original cast member of the Broadway show *Rent*. It was a pretty big deal to meet all these interesting people during those early days. I had never had any real-life interactions with celebrities at that point. I still vividly remember nervously gulping down water and choking on sushi in front of Rapp.

I started living a bit of a double life after teaming up with my business partner, Stephen Lucin. He had started his own PR company as well. Pretty soon, I'd find myself going back and forth to New York City daily. I worked during the day at my job but felt uninspired.

The firm was great, and I was truly grateful for the opportunity, but I couldn't help thinking of what other adventures might be in front of me if I was fully in control of my destiny. At night, I would party it up or escort clients to events, watching Grapevine PR grow, and having a blast while doing it. Even though there wasn't much money coming in yet, the risks I took were well rewarded! I was not done rolling the dice, though. There was limitless potential.

It was time for the narrative around Grapevine PR to change. The story had to reflect the values, *Roots*, and truth of its founders. We made it public that Grapevine PR was gay-owned.

Branding ourselves as an LGBTQ-focused PR firm, we were concentrating on representing LGBTQ-identifying clients, such as authors, musicians, independent filmmakers, and businesses. By September 2007, we already had a dozen clients and started promoting ourselves to the media. Most clients were pro bono or getting our services at a steal, but I loved every minute of it.

Grapevine PR was destined for something more. I could feel it. The company could grow only so much while I was chained to the desk of my day job. The solution was simple. Pitch our story to the largest newspaper in New Jersey. That would help Grapevine, no doubt about it. The problem was my daytime gig at the PR firm. If you worked there, you couldn't have your own PR firm on the side. Oh, and did I mention that my boss religiously read that paper every day to keep tabs on his firm's own clients and trends?

It was a sizable risk, but I felt compelled. Grapevine PR's story fucking mattered.

In fact, it mattered so much that it ended up being featured on the front page of the business section with my own face on it. Great news for Grapevine PR and a guarantee my boss would see the story and promptly fire me. But I was ready to take that leap.

BUSINESS

Steve Le Vine of Freehold says that in addition to serving entertainers, grapeVine Public Relations will educate the public about gay-related issues, such as young people who have been thrown out of their homes because of their sexual orientation. (PHOTO: JERRY WOLKOWITZ, SPECIAL TO THE PRESS)

Area gay-oriented publicity firm sees opportunity in acceptance

2 friends join forces, focus on entertainment, civic service

By NICK PETRUNCIO
FREEHOLD BUREAU

Public relations is all about relationships, and PR professionals Steve Le Vine and Stephen Lucin want to introduce a niche market to what they see as an increasingly accepting mass audience.

The two friends, who are both 25, have formed grapeVine Public Relations, a firm that provides publicity for entertainers who are lesbian, gay, bisexual, transgender (LGBT) or friendly to those groups and that also tries to educate the public about issues such as homeless young people who have been thrown out of their homes because of their sexual orientation.

"It hasn't really been done before. It's very rare," said Le Vine about the firm.

Le Vine, who grew up in Freehold and graduated from Freehold High School, and Lucin, who is originally from Bergen County, both graduated from William Patterson University in Wayne.

> "We're both openly gay, so it was like a natural thing because we both understand the market."
>
> — Steve Le Vine

Le Vine has worked in public relations at various firms in New Jersey and then went into business for himself, forming grapeVine Public Relations, focusing mostly on music and entertainment publicity.

Since graduating, Lucin has worked in journalism and public relations, most recently working in PR in Los Angeles. He previously managed SJL Public Relations in Bergen County and focused more on civic service and organizational PR.

The clients at both their respective firms were gay or gay-friendly, so they decided to merge into one firm under the grapeVine name, focusing on both entertainment and civic service in the LGBT community.

"We're both openly gay, so it was like a natural thing because we both understand the market," Le Vine said.

Their business is in the early stages, and they will have a kick-off party Sept. 28 at Splash Bar in Manhattan. Some of their clients will perform and will do a meet-and-greet, said Le Vine, who added that the LGBT support center in the city will be on hand to address the issue of homeless youth in the community.

GrapeVine had five clients at last count, and the two have been in negotiations to acquire more, Le Vine said. The credits of their current clients include TV shows like "Law & Order" and "Guiding Light," movies like "A Tale of Two Pizzas" with Vincent Pastore and Frank Vincent of "The Sopranos," off-Broadway productions like "Jewtopia," and appearances on Comedy Central and Caroline's Comedy Club.

The two represent Freehold mystery author Gil

Visit our Web site, www.app.com, and click on this story in the Business section for a link to:
grapeVine.

Burgess, who wrote "Dead of Winter," and Outivities, a new gay social activities organization that is expected to be launched soon.

The two don't have a permanent office just yet; their business is still in the early stages, Le Vine said. But downtown Freehold is one of the locations they are considering, he said.

"We just want to make sure that in our lifetime that sexuality doesn't matter," and what is important is a person's accomplishments, not his or her personal life, Lucin said.

The firm can be reached at (732) 616-5545.

Nick Petruncio. (732) 308-7752 or npetruncio@app.com

THE ADVOCATE

Hey, Flack, Watch Your Back

BY CHRIS GARDNER

In Hollywood it's easier to name publicists who aren't gay rather than single out the ones who are. But two young flacks have partnered up to make a name for themselves as cofounders of GrapeVine Public Relations—perhaps the first firm to specifically serve gay and gay-friendly actors, writers, and musicians.

Steven Le Vine and Stephen Lucin are the brains behind the company, which boasts talent like tranny superstar Amanda Lepore (pictured), actor Michael Carbonaro (*Another Gay Movie*), and comedian Jason Stuart. The firm has also been involved with events like the Philadelphia International Gay & Lesbian Film Festival, MIX NYC, and NewFest.

Le Vine and Lucin—both in their mid 20s and recent college grads—hope to attract talent through a targeted strategy. "[Gay clients] know we understand them better than a regular firm," says Le Vine. "There's also been a lot of talk that gay media outlets are consolidating because the gay market is merging with the mainstream press, so that leaves a lot of gay celebs in the middle."

One client they may have a hard time finding a place for is Carbonaro, known for his raunchy role in *Another Gay Movie*, since the queer-friendly actor declines to discuss his sexual orientation in the media. But Le Vine and Lucin insist that working with gay clients is just a specialty, not a mandate. Says Lucin: "If they're worried about it, we will work with them in different ways."

Le Vine sees GrapeVine evolving into "an entertainment firm that hosts events and parties, not just for the fun factor but also to raise awareness and money for issues facing the LGBT community, especially homeless gay youth." Lucin adds, "I'm gay and Steven's gay, and we should give back somehow."

All my family and friends warned me I was risking my entire career. That going off on my own was tantamount to craziness. That I had lost my mind and was being irresponsible. Deep down, I knew it was the right move. So, I followed my gut instinct.

A few days later, I found myself in the HR office. They seemed utterly bewildered, but I was prepared. Possibly even a little cocky. The conversation went a little something like this:

HR: "So…Is it true that you have your *own* PR firm?"

Me: "Yup."

HR: "Well, you can't work here if you have your own PR company. You're competing with us."

Me: "We have different kinds of clients, though."

HR: "It doesn't matter. You could still be competition. You need to decide if you want to work here and give up your company or not."

Me: "I've put so much effort into this over the last few months. This is my baby. And I would always regret it if I didn't go after my dream and continue with it. So do what you have to do."

Getting fired was the best thing that ever happened to me. It was on my own terms. Don't get me wrong, it wasn't smooth sailing. The odds were stacked against me. My family and friends were all against it. Heck, even the economy played hardball. But it was a risk I had to take for Grapevine to flourish.

I was finally following my passion. Grapevine started to sign more clients, and I moved to Los Angeles the following year in my beat-up Chevy Camaro. I was a 26-year-old trying to survive and keep Grapevine PR going amidst the economic collapse of 2008. It was a risk I needed to take, and Grapevine PR blossomed as a result, even if I had to eat canned tuna every day for lunch and dinner.

Years later, I'd end up working with clients like Monte Pittman, Madonna's longtime guitarist and killer rock 'n roll and metal musician. In 2012, I had the opportunity to join Monte on Madonna's MDNA Tour throughout Europe, and nearly a decade later, got the chance to join my client, the supremely talented conscious hip-hop artist, Souleye, on his wife Alanis Morissette's Jagged Little Pill 25th Anniversary Tour. I also got the opportunity to travel overseas to various countries in Africa a half dozen times with clients.

On Madonna's tourbus in Berlin after the MDNA show, July 2012

Best of all, I got to work with my father's hero, William Shatner, Grammy-winning singer-songwriter Lisa Loeb (another personal favorite artist of mine), and many other amazing people. Grapevine grew into an established Hollywood PR firm, something it never would have been if I stayed chained to my desk at my 9-5. Understanding the level of *Stakes* and overcoming them was critical to the recipe that fueled Grapevine's early growth.

Steven with Grapevine PR client William Shatner in his office in 2017

Steven with client Lisa Loeb behind-the-scenes during a promotional shoot, 2019

6

IMPACT: YOUR SOLUTION, PRODUCT, OR IDEA

mpact is what separates good stories from stories that fucking matter. *Impact* makes your promises, outcomes, and effects clear to your target audience. It gives them a simple, straightforward understanding of how they will benefit from your solution or vision.

You've managed to hold your audience's attention with a compelling origin story and riveting *Stakes*, but what is the next storytelling step? After covering your *Roots* and *Stakes*, it is time to focus on the way you are making an impact. Your audience wants to know how they can engage with you, and they need a call to action.

Remember, the media landscape's cacophony of noise can easily swallow up your story. That's where the final pillar of an STFM comes in.

Impact is a simple but powerful concept. It adds magic to our storytelling that *Roots* and *Stakes* cannot: It gives your audience a reason to care. There are real-world examples of this all around us. Supreme, Versace, Patagonia, and Zara all gave their audiences a reason to care, and their success can attest to that.

Take Zara, for example. It is a brand that adapts quickly, and they communicate this in various ways, always placing the customer at the core. To pull this off, you need to know your audience really well. Regardless of how unique their audiences are, these brands wield their storytelling impactfully.

The secret is determining the *Impact* and making it relatable. Identifying your *Impact* can be a struggle sometimes, but this tip may prove useful. Put yourself in your audience's shoes and ask, "What's in it for me?" I'll explain by using the baby food example from the previous chapter.

Let's say the founders of this brand put themselves in their audience's shoes. How is their audience benefiting? Is the baby food organic? Is the company supporting small farmers in its community? Is its supply chain green and sustainable? What is the bigger picture here?

Whatever *your* solution, your audience needs to know what's in it for them. That's how you maintain interest and continue to build on that foundation of trust, which is essential.

We want to share stories with our audience about who we are helping because it evokes emotions and makes a story much more memorable. This is how we build a following and help our audience relate to our brand. We want our storytelling to stick, and each pillar of an STFM is aimed at making this happen.

Evoking emotion builds trust in one's audience, and storytellers can aim for specific emotions to heighten the impact. Social proof can help you home in on and truly understand how your audience connects with and relates to your story. Let's take a closer look.

Let's use popular footwear brand Allbirds as an example. Let's say they wanted to figure out their own story using our STFM model.

Their Roots: It was founded by professional soccer player Tim Brown. He played for the Newcastle Jets and Wellington Phoenix, but retired in 2012. Brown pursued his interests, which led to the formation of Allbirds.

Their Stakes: Using new materials for their footwear and being eco-friendly and budget-friendly in the process. It's a risky business to incorporate new or alternative materials in shoes. So many things can go wrong. The stitching might tear. The design might not hold up to performance standards. The materials might be too expensive. But Allbirds has integrated new and alternative materials into their footwear product line successfully.

Once Allbirds has *Roots* and *Stakes* nailed down, they can then take a look at the *Impact* they are making. Their *Impact* would focus on what makes Allbirds' solution unique and how it is helping others. In Allbirds' case, they might choose to highlight that their trail running shoes are made from castor oil-based foam or that their approach to designing and manufacturing is different and eco-friendly.

Key takeaway: The stronger your audience can identify with the *Impact* you are making, the more convincing your story becomes. This is what ultimately leads them to enroll in your vision and solution.

The "Right" Story to Tell - Choose Wisely

Impact is more than a buzzword. *Impact* tells us how a person's solution is changing the world. It implies causality. Simply saying, "we made a difference," and hoping for the best won't cut it.

Time and again, purpose-driven brands make the same mistake: They are too busy to measure the success of their story. Investing in your company's ability to identify and share stories behind your program, product, or solution can be one of the strongest and most cost-effective strategies to communicate and measure the power of your *Impact*. Here's why:

- *Stories make quantitative data (data measured with quantifiable numbers) easier to relate to, giving it a human face.*
- *Stories are not passive or one-sided. They offer the audience a chance to digest and retain information much more easily.*
- *Stories are excellent vehicles for rebranding, distilling change that's been taking place over long periods into a cohesive narrative.*
- *Stories can help to foster a sense of pride and belonging in your brand's stakeholders, making them effective tools to measure the qualitative impact (qualitative data is measured using qualities or words rather than numbers).*

Smart nonprofits make use of their *Impact* pillar in revolutionary ways. They tend to approach storytelling a bit more strategically than other types of organizations, considering how their narrative aligns with the goals of their organization and how their audience may engage with it.

Choosing the right story hinges on how you answer these questions:

Is your ideal outcome an increased awareness or understanding of an issue or cause? Nonprofits frequently use stories to increase awareness on issues like better access to education, protection for domestic abuse survivors, climate change, or women's health.

Do you aim to shift perceptions or societal attitudes? A popular storytelling technique used here is the "day in the life" approach. The goal here is to foster familiarity with the target audience by showing them a different angle on the story. Nigel Ng Kin-ju (Uncle Roger), with his bright orange polo, is no stranger to this form of storytelling. The comedian uses this approach exceptionally well to share what a day in the life of his over-the-top persona is like. The approach was so successful that it shot Nigel Ng from obscurity to stardom in a matter of months.

Are you hoping to bring a community together to demystify a process, product, or service? Entire communities are built around different brands, solutions, and topics. Your story should make it clear how your contribution to the community is different. Successful books often strive to demystify a topic. Just take a look at all those books on crypto investing. Some of the most successful books in that genre take complex ideas and explain them simply.

At the very core of the matter, choosing the right story stems from having a deep understanding of why a story should be told and to whom it matters.

Assessing Your Story's Impact

Indicators are useful to help us assess the power or effectiveness of your story. Indicators also provide valuable data, which enables us to adapt the story whenever needed. Some indicators are more useful than others when ascertaining if a story has had a tangible impact. Consider monitoring the following indicators in your next campaign:

- *Sign-ups for your initiatives, products, or events.*
- *The tone and quality of conversations within a community (social listening is useful here).*
- *Dollars raised. This can be through increased sales, donations, or funding.*
- *Downloads or purchases of a resource.*
- *The engagement (views, shares, likes, comments) with the story on social media.*

When we know how an audience reacts to a story, it becomes so much easier to tweak it for better results. These indicators, when monitored thoroughly, can help us grow the power of our story while imparting precious insights that could influence future storytelling decisions.

Don't get too caught up in the data, though. There is richness in the tradition of storytelling, which means the quickest path to producing a convincing outcomes-based narrative may not be straightforward. The balance between effective communication and the need to tell an authentic story needs to be maintained. Think of storytelling as a data-informed activity rather than being entirely data-driven (Digital Storytellers, 2021).

Tips to Craft Impactful Stories to Win Headlines and Hearts

The basics of epic storytelling are much easier to pull off than you think. While the thought of crafting a rousing narrative may elicit a groan and shudders of deadline stress, the truth is you don't need to be a wordsmith to tell a good fucking story. Humans are natural storytellers, after all! With a little refinement, those stories can evolve into something more compelling.

Finish With Data: A common mistake storytellers tend to make is to include loads of data. Data is useful, but stuffing a story with statistics will not increase its influence. The numbers should never overshadow the human element. It would be far more efficient to hook your audience with a story that has tension, emotion, and conflict. Your goal is to make your audience feel something, followed by supporting metrics.

Root for the Underdog: The most powerful way to tell brand stories is through the perspective of one person's journey. This person can be a brand representative or other stakeholder, but the key lies in picking a story rich in detail and drama. A story that adds backbone to the "why" of your brand. When we focus on a single person, their story becomes more relatable and the impact your solution has becomes easier to grasp.

Power Lives in the Details: Little details can bring a story to life and make it easier to recall. Remember, a good story engages our senses, and details about the setting, mood, and characters are all important. Your audience wants to know what things look like, good or bad (such as the excitement in the eyes of a child receiving toys or the destruction that a Category 5 hurricane left behind). So always be on the lookout for the little details that can bring a story to life and add a human touch to it.

Interview Like Lois Lane: There's a reason why Lois Lane was the star reporter for the Daily Planet in the Superman comics. She asked a lot of questions, and you should, too. You'll get a lot of answers that will help you shape your story. Use direct quotes from people you have interviewed (and who are relevant to the story). You'll be surprised at the gems that can turn up!

Keep It Conversational and Light: There's a reason why some college professors can talk us to sleep, even on the most jovial of topics. It is the language they use! Overly formal language and jargon sap the life out of a story, but so does doomsday messaging. Often, marketing and storytelling fall into the trap of painting a dark and gloomy future. While it may work in the short term, it is not an effective long-term solution. People want to hear stories of hope, of a brighter future. They want transformative change to inspire them. Keeping the tone of your story conversational, punchy, and positive will go a long way in improving your storytelling.

Identifying Your Most Powerful Story

There's a reason why Steve Jobs' Stanford commencement address is almost always included in a list of influential speeches. The address is incredibly moving, thanks to all the impactful stories it contains, making it a favorite for many. People love to hear stories like this, but very few are comfortable delivering them. That's because these stories expose our flaws and lay bare the struggles we've been through. These struggles are what make stories inspiring, so there's no need to cringe or feel exposed. Not sharing them is a missed opportunity. There are some effective techniques for unearthing these powerful stories.

Memory Recall to Trigger Stories

Most people try to recall memories chronologically when developing their stories, but there is another more effective way to conjure up those deep, dormant stores. Grab a notepad and pencil and jot down the details for the following:

People: Make a mind map. Write your brand's name in the middle of the paper and start drawing out relationships (stakeholders, family, friends). Each time you draw a connecting line between your brand's name and people, think through the relationship dynamics and emotions. There's a story waiting to be uncovered in these connections.

Places: When recalling places that matter, don't be afraid to get specific. Whether it is that brief talk you had with the teacher in your child's middle school, or a road trip last summer, retracing your steps will help to dust off long-buried memories and forgotten interactions.

Things: Objects can have symbolic meaning (gifts, awards, books, medals, etc.). Try to recall which items hold symbolic meaning for you. If it was a medal, trophy, or award for some type of achievement, try to reflect on what motivated you to obtain that reward.

When you are done fleshing out the people, places, and things significant to your brand, you'll likely notice story kernels. Taking your story planning a step further, write down single-line summaries of each story kernel. Some stories may be too personal to share, but they can contain useful anecdotes that can be used to craft a narrative that matters.

Once you've brainstormed a host of stories that can be used in different types of situations, it would be best practice to catalog these stories for easy access. Use whatever categorization makes sense for you.

Refining the Angle

A well-crafted and precise positioning statement is a powerful tool to bring focus and clarity to your story that matters. If used properly, this statement can help to differentiate your solution from the competition and attract audience members. There are several criteria you need to look at when checking your brand position, i.e., the angle of your story. Work your way through the checklist below whenever you need to check your brand positioning.

- *Does the positioning statement come from a place of abundance and growth (this is the solution we offer) rather than a place of scarcity and lack (stop doing X, or else!)?*
- *Does the statement match your target audience's views of your brand or solution?*
- *Does the positioning statement set your solution apart from the competition?*
- *Is your solution's unique value identified in the statement?*
- *Does it focus on your target audience?*
- *Is the statement memorable, motivating, and easy to understand?*

Positioning is not something you "do." It is the impression your actions leave on the target audience. It's your job to make that impression a good one. Your positioning statement and tagline should communicate how you want your solution to be represented. Brands that manage to cut through the noise tend to merge their passion with their positioning into a single statement.

Positioning Strategies

Solopreneurs thrive on reputations. Every day, our storytelling is influencing the target audience's perceptions. Positioning helps your storytelling stay relevant to your audience, which leads to higher conversion rates and return on investment. Several types of position strategies can be employed to this end.

Quality of Service: Spotlighting the quality of customer service. This becomes doubly important if your prices are higher than your competitors. The target audience will need to know why the price difference is justified.

Price: Pricing will influence how your target audience views your brand, ultimately influencing how your brand is positioned. For audiences on a budget, consider homing in on great service that won't burn a hole in the customer's pocket. On the other hand, certain audiences expect to pay more for certain goods and services and associate higher prices with luxury. It all boils down to knowing what your audience is willing to spend on your solution.

Convenience: With this positioning strategy, the goal is to demonstrate why your solution is more convenient than the competition.

Niche Service: Are your solutions providing products or services that aren't widely available? Spotlighting your uniqueness is usually the best approach to differentiating yourself from others.

Problem and Solution: It may be worth focusing the angle of your storytelling on the theme of "powerful solutions" if it addresses a problem many people have. Whether it's a cookbook, webinar, or something else, the solution should be immediate and actionable.

Using Storytelling to Sell Your Vision

When we give away our best information without any stories to back it up, it will likely result in a lukewarm reception. Danny Pintauro's story went viral because it made the audience feel something. People remember how you make them feel, not the data you feed them. As a solopreneur or expert, you need your audience to buy into your vision. For that to happen, they need to remember you first. Fortunately, stories are your key. I'll share the basic formula behind memorable storytelling.

Present Your Solution Simply: With your solution, the point you want your audience to understand should be direct and simple (Keuilian, 2018). This is the "hook" of your story. An excellent hook will be a one- to two-sentence summary of your larger story. Think of it as your story's teaser, similar to how a teaser for a new film might try to get people to see the full movie. Its name describes exactly what it intends to do: to "hook" people in.

Back-Up Your Point: After you've made your point, you should seek to back it up and explain why it matters. Here's an example:

Leadership is the problem and the solution. Five years ago, I always had problems with my employees. The ones who weren't trying to sabotage me were doing lazy work. At the time, I was convinced it was a testament to their character. Boy, was I wrong! The penny dropped when I was on vacation with my family. I was allowing sloppy standards. I was being too timid as a leader. The vacation was cut short, and I made changes that were needed. Higher expectations were established and enforced, and my employee problems would become a thing of the past.

Use Metaphors and Similes: Metaphors and similes are used to demonstrate the point (your solution) again, but from a different perspective. Metaphors and similes are powerful tools to help illustrate complex ideas.

Quick English lesson refresher: both similes and metaphors are figurative speech. A simile makes a comparison by saying one thing is *like* something else (*Life* is like *a box of chocolates*), whereas a metaphor makes a comparison by saying one thing *is* something else (*Life* is *but a dream*).

Let's add a simile to the above example about leadership and see how it pans out.

Leadership is a lot like rowing a boat. You need to have both oars in the water, otherwise, you'll end up going in circles.

The repetitive structure of the formula is designed to help your audience remember your story easily. When we understand the angle of the story we want to pitch to our audience, it gives us an idea of how we want to position it to them.

7

———

SOCIAL PROOF

Understanding Social Proof

Have you ever wondered why some people are bombarded with opportunities while others are overlooked? One book proposal is relegated to the bin, while publishers fight over another one. The same thing can be seen in our personal lives as well. One person always struggles to find a date, while another receives non-stop propositions despite being in a relationship. Social proof is behind all of this.

When we regard a person or business as successful, that view tends to spread, but in the absence of social proof, people are more attentive to flaws and become more dismissive. Two personal development writers can be equally talented, but one will have trouble getting published—the writer who does not have a book on a bestseller list.

The impact of social proof goes beyond denying and offering opportunities. It can have a very tangible effect on human behavior. The Arizona Petrified Forest is a perfect example of this. Some visitors perhaps thought that the unusual, petrified wood might make an interesting keepsake. In any case, the theft of petrified wood got so bad that the staff put up a sign. It read: "Your heritage is being vandalized every day by theft losses of petrified wood of fourteen tons a year, mostly a small piece at a time" (Bernheimer, 2019). The sign was intended to deter theft, but it had the opposite effect. The depletion of petrified wood increased, if not tripled. It turns out the sign served as social proof. Everyone was stealing petrified wood chips, so it must be considered acceptable behavior, right?

Another example of social proof can be found in the theaters and opera houses of old. They were claqueurs, otherwise known as "professional applauders." Their job is to applaud the performance and encourage others to do the same, giving audience members a more positive view of the experience. While claqueurs are a dying breed, their existence shows that social proof has been used to mold the tastes of an uncertain audience since ancient times.

Professional applauders have been around since the theater of Dionysus hosted performances in ancient Athens. In 4th century BC comedy competitions, Philemon would frequently wipe the floor with his rival Menander. Menander was by no means an inferior playwright; Philemon just proved to be a better strategist. Philemon would have claqueurs infiltrate the audience to sway the decision of the judges (Britannica, T. Editors of Encyclopaedia, 2019). Everyone laughed and applauded, encouraged by claqueurs, giving the impression that Philemon's plays were superior.

Savvy business owners have been using social proof for years to attract a wider audience. Here are some real-world examples of how social proof is used:

- The party crowd in New York is familiar with queues at clubs that snake around the block. These queues are there by design. Making patrons wait outside nightclubs and bars increases the perception that the venue is popular. This increases the likelihood of attracting passersby.
- TV shows make use of canned laughter and recorded sound to enhance the perception of applaudable and funny situations. It is pretty much a modern version of claqueurs.
- Fast food chains display signs of how many people or meals they serve. McDonald's sign "Billions and Billions Served" comes to mind here.

Types Of Social Proof

Social proof is everywhere, but it is nothing new. People have been following the advice and recommendations of their contemporaries for centuries. Social proof provides better visibility for your brand, but its true goal should not be undermined—to build a bond of trust between your brand and its target audience. Fortunately, there are several ways we can go about forging that bond.

The Power of Testimonials, Case Studies, Logos, and Spotlights

Testimonials (especially from customers) are worth their weight in gold. If your business leans towards a consultative sales process, you may want to consider using a detailed case study as a testimonial. This will illustrate how your solution will benefit the customer. You may also want to consider having a spotlight section on your website to highlight customer success stories.

For businesses leaning towards a transactional sales process, sprinkle customer testimonials throughout your website, especially at the point of sale. The customer testimonials should ideally be in the form of short quotes that address sales objections.

Another way you can improve your brand's social proof is to set up a "happy customer page" that shows off real people that love your product. This can have a powerful impact, especially if you provide services to other businesses or blue-chip clients. Displaying their logo on your "happy customer" page can help to boost your brand's credibility.

Showing off your happy and satisfied customers in ads and emails and on your website and landing pages is a fantastic way of using social proof to increase conversations. In fact, testimonials can generate 62% more revenue from customers who visit your site (Roth, n.d.).

The Double-Edged Sword of Press Mentions

The media is a fickle beast, but positive coverage can expose your brand to a much larger audience. It shows that your brand is worthy of attention, especially if the mention comes from a popular outlet. There are two surefire ways to get your brand mentioned in the media. The first method is the most budget-friendly one. Earn your keep in the press with a story that fucking matters—it will be worth all that blood, sweat, and tears.

I am not a fan of the second method: Buying exposure. Yes, it can help you rank better in search engine results, but it is costly and comes with an annoying *"sponsored content"* tag. Sponsored content has a huge trust problem and creates confusion and feelings of deception in one's target audience (Lazauskas, 2014). In other words, sponsored content has the potential to undo all the hard work you've done to earn your audience's trust!

Publishers assume readers know that "sponsored content" means that an advertiser paid for the article and influenced the content. Education levels also have an interesting influence on people's willingness to trust sponsored content. Typically, the higher your target audience's education level, the less trust they will place in it. Tread this route carefully, and don't let "good press" snake-oil salesmen burn a hole in your pocket.

Customer Activity Notifications in Real Time

This trend in social proof marketing requires customer activity to be displayed on your website. It can be as simple as displaying how many people have visited the site, enrolled in a course, or made purchases. QVC has been doing this for ages. Sometimes websites have little pop-ups declaring something along the lines of: *"Suzie from Boston bought Product X five minutes ago!"* The purpose of these pop-ups and visitor numbers is simple. It is the online version of those queues outside New York clubs.

Using Social Proof to Reach New Audiences

As long as the media has been around, brands have used social proof to create the impression that their solutions are hot property. Before the Internet connected an entire planet, the only way to find out what consumers really thought was through low-tech means like reading consumer magazines and phone surveys. The Internet changed all of that. We have social proof available at our fingertips, but it must be used wisely. This means you'll need to:

Know The Purpose: Social proof can be impactful when it is the last thing someone reads before making a decision, or it can be used in top-of-funnel marketing and in the research stage. Wherever you decide to use social proof, its purpose has to remain clear.

Weave Social Proof Naturally Into Your Story: Social proof should benefit your storytelling approach and be logically incorporated into website navigation (Berg, 2022).

Be Strategic: Carefully consider the right moment to deliver social proof to create a positive impact on your audience. It should fit into your storytelling experience, giving your audience the most critical elements of information they need to make a decision.

There are several ways you can effectively use social proof to build trust with your target audience. Here are some of the most beneficial strategies to use:

Use Experts On Your Socials

Inviting experts to take the reins of your brand's social media platforms can be extremely successful. Experts in any field can carry weight with followers in that group. The authority and trust they have already established make their support for your brand more credible, thanks to the halo effect. The halo effect, in essence, is a cognitive bias in which our overall impression of a person or company influences how we think and feel about that person or company (Cherry, 2020). For example, "That expert is saying good things about Jennifer and her puppy training company. If that expert thinks Jennifer and her company are likable and trustworthy, then she must be. Therefore, I should trust and buy from Jennifer and her puppy training company."

We know this first-hand from when one nutraceutical client of ours engaged a top nutrition specialist to serve as its chief spokesperson to provide media interviews, publish content, and appear at industry conventions. By doing so, the brand's credibility was strengthened, and its position within its marketplace was further elevated.

Spotlight Earned Mentions

Showing gratitude for your media mentions is a beautiful way of using social proof to spotlight your success. This approach needs some tact to come across as an accomplishment and not a boast. Sharing your gratitude for customer shout-outs is also a good idea for helping build trust. You don't have to go as far as Slack did (they created a Twitter account just for their mentions), but a little creativity and gratitude go a long way.

8

LEVERAGE YOUR STORY TO MAKE HEADLINES

Once you have established your story, defined your target audience, and done the work to position it, you have now created the perfect opportunity to leverage it to gain substantial press coverage in top newspapers and magazines, and on popular TV and radio programs. Why? Because you've executed an effective earned media strategy.

The Power of Earned Media

Ethics and trust in the media are crucial, and the public has the right to know what content has been paid for and what has been earned on its own merit. Journalists, PR professionals, and members of the media are expected to uphold professional standards and respect the boundary between paid, earned, and owned media.

Let's discuss what constitutes each of these categories:

Earned Media: Attention generated through media outreach, otherwise known as publicity (or PR). Its sole purpose is to entice reporters, journalists, producers, and other members of the media to cover your story. No money should be exchanged between a journalist and an individual conducting media outreach. Make no mistake: earned media can be difficult to obtain and very time-consuming, but the value outweighs any of this as it can generate substantial positive press coverage at a fraction of the cost of advertising.

Owned Media: This involves all the content you create and control and can include anything from YouTube videos to your latest article on LinkedIn or Medium. Owned media can overlap with earned media when it includes something like an op-ed piece or a guest-contributed byline article that you wrote but is placed in someone else's publication. The good thing is that you generally don't need to worry about censorship with owned media, which means your message can be communicated how you intended it. The exception is when content is published in someone else's media outlet. The downside is that your story-telling may lack a significant audience and could be considered biased since it lacks the third-party credibility that comes with being written about by someone else.

Paid Media: This route involves paying for media placements, such as advertisements, which are more visual and promotional. Advertorials (paid media meant to look like editorial pieces) and placements (a news article or byline article) are fair game in this practice. It can also include owned media when social media advertising is used. In most cases, paid and earned media should work in harmony to bolster marketing and branding efforts, but paid media comes with an enormous downside. This route tends to be extremely costly and can easily leach tens or even hundreds of thousands of dollars out of your budget for consistent and optimal results. Also, paid media is not as persuasive as earned media.

Typically, paid media can be spotted by its "sponsored post" tag. Ethical media outlets use this to let the public know that a piece of content was paid for. One of the most common uses for paid media (and the reason why its credibility is poor) is its use in advertising. Big brands make use of it all the time, but remember, the world loves a scandal and does not easily forget if a brand tricked them. A study found that the vast majority of consumers (94%) will remain loyal to a completely transparent brand (Hyken, 2019). The same study also found that most consumers would be willing to fork over more money for goods and services from a transparent brand. Despite this fact, some brands try to get ahead with misleading and false information.

Big companies are not immune to the temptation of spreading misleading claims through paid media. Remember Dannon and their Activia yogurt? We've already ascertained that advertisements fall into the paid media bracket. Dannon specifically marketed the yogurt as "clinically and scientifically proven" to regulate digestion and boost a person's immune system. It was priced 30% above the competitors' products and even featured a television ad campaign with Jamie Lee Curtis. Dannon realized their faux pas a little too late when a consumer took them to court over the marketing claims. The consumer had stomach problems and, persuaded by the ad, purchased the product. She observed no difference in her condition, and a class action lawsuit followed. Dannon was fined $21 million and had to remove the words "clinically" and "scientifically proven" from their labels (Jurberg, 2020).

Unless you want your brand's storytelling to give your audience indigestion, it is best to steer clear of paid media's dark side. Earned media can build credibility, visibility, awareness, and trust, but paid media can undo all your hard work if shady ethics are at play.

Developing Your EPK

Earned media outreach becomes a bit easier once you have developed your brand's Electronic Press Kit (EPK), which you can share with the media. An EPK is a digital promotional package that contains your brand's most important elements and foundational assets and can prove as a highly effective tool to have when launching or maintaining an ongoing PR campaign. It can exist as a neatly laid out guide, a password-protected section of your website, or even a collection of raw assets in a folder on Dropbox, Google Drive, or a flash drive. The way you store it is not important—the contents reign supreme here.

A well-thought-out EPK will properly present journalists, producers, and other media personnel with essential information and multimedia assets for them to keep on hand or to pull whenever they are covering you and your brand. You can also physically display your EPK when appearing at conventions, trade shows, keynote speeches, and other "in-person" events for reporters to take with them when considering potential future coverage. At a minimum, your Electronic Press Kit should contain the following:

Key Bios: Biographies about all key team members or just yourself.

Headshots and Marketing Images: Photographs from the shoulders up (headshots) and those that help tell a story (editorial or marketing shots), along with proper photo credits.

Backgrounder: Detailed information about your company and core products.

Round out your EPK with a killer boilerplate that focuses on consistent messaging relating to your brand. Your boilerplate should address the five key questions on every reporter's lips: Who, what, when, where, and why. The function of a boilerplate is to tell the reader in a condensed and straightforward manner what is most important and compelling about your brand. It is usually no longer than a single paragraph. Boilerplate text does more than tease journalists with a possible story idea; it adds credibility to your EPK and gives interested parties a way to contact you (Brown, 2018). Writing a knockout boilerplate takes time, patience, and practice, but these steps will help smooth the process along.

Determine the Angle

Keep in mind, you have 100 words or less to describe your business. Fortunately, these can be written in many different ways. Some may choose to highlight information that aligns with their business goals, brand image, company culture, or investors. Others may choose, however, to spotlight recent accolades or accomplishments. While none of these angles are "wrong," it is important to decide beforehand what the goal of your EPK will be. Tailor your boilerplate around this goal.

Describe Your Business

Boilerplates can be used to effectively attract attention when details like a brand's impact, revenue, growth, and relevance are addressed. If a journalist reads your boilerplate, they need to glean all the critical information they would need regarding your brand. It's a tall order, considering the limited word count! To clearly and concisely communicate what your brand is about, start by writing a short (one- or two-sentence) description based on your value prop. That way, you'll be able to filter out unnecessary details and only keep to the most important bits. Think of it as a condensed version of the "About" page on your website.

Once you have this part of your description down pat, it's time to focus on other elements to add to the boilerplate, namely:

- The industry in which your business falls into
- What your business does
- With who you are working
- Where your business is located
- When your brand was founded
- Company size
- Market share
- Mission and vision statement
- Awards or accolades received

This seems like a lot to cram into 100 words or less, but it can be done. In fact, Lyft did this effortlessly with 65 words!

"Lyft was founded in June 2012 by Logan Green and John Zimmer to reconnect people and communities through better transportation. Lyft is the fastest-growing rideshare company in the U.S. and is available in more than 190 cities. Lyft is preferred by drivers and passengers for its safe and friendly experience and its commitment to driving positive change for the future of our cities," (Lyft, 2016).

Call to Action

At the end of your EPK, a call to action is needed. This can be as simple as providing a link to your websites and social media accounts, inviting the reader to take a specific action by following you.

Provide Contact Details

An EPK is useless without contact information. You will want members of the media to be able to reach you or a representative for more information or even to schedule an interview to cover your story. Make sure to include a phone number and email address at the very end of your kit. Use the primary contact details for your business; you don't want to miss a potential interview with an interested reporter!

Building a Target Media List

One of the key components of executing a successful media relations campaign is identifying the media outlets and specific journalists to which you are conducting outreach. If you don't have the answer to this, then your PR campaign is dead in the water, in the same way you first needed to adequately define your brand's target audience in order to successfully pitch them on your products, services, or solutions.

The trick to doing so is to create your target media list. First, start with broad details and then dive deeper. Don't be afraid to get granular throughout this process, as there are so many media outlets and reporters to choose from. Knowing the difference between a consumer and a trade media outlet will go a long way in helping you target the appropriate channel for telling your story. Let's take a look at the distinction between both.

The Skinny on Consumer and Trade Media

Next time you are in the grocery store, pay attention to the magazines at the checkout line. Most likely, familiar titles like *Rolling Stone* and *Men's Health* come to mind. These magazines are what we call consumer media, and usually this form of media has a dedicated website where consumers can read more content.

As you've already guessed, consumer magazines are aimed at the general public. They have an impressively large audience and are considered general interest magazines. However, titles like *Rolling Stone* and *Redbook* are considered specialized publications as well since they focus on specific areas. Consumer magazines can be purchased either as one-offs or through a monthly, quarterly, or annual subscription. There are a multitude of outlets, all focusing on different genres such as lifestyle, business, health and wellness, entertainment, finance, and technology. Just go into any Barnes & Noble and check out the magazines section, and you'll be shocked at how many magazines are published and available to the public.

Trade media is quite different. Think of *Packaging World* or the *Oil and Gas Journal.* These publications are targeted toward specific industries and professions and cover topics that are predominantly relevant to those working in the field or adjacent ones. Often, trade media is referred to as "trade journals" or "trades" and aims to offer news and information, byline content, studies, interviews, and feature articles. As with consumer media, trade journals often have a website connected to the magazine as well.

Since trades focus on specific industries or trade niches, these types of media are described as places where people can go to "talk shop" and discover new trends in a particular profession. These magazines are often only available by subscription. Content is written by staff editors, but trades are known to hire freelancers as it is cost-effective (Forde,

2018). Trade media typically have budget constraints due to their small but loyal audiences.

The granular process begins when you are piecing your target media list together. You'll need to pin down where your story will fit. When compiling your target media list, take the time to include the following details:

- The reporter or producer's name
- The media outlet's name
- The frequency of publication of the outlet.
- The outlet or contact's area of coverage (i.e., DMA - Designated Market Area)
- The reporter or producer's role (i.e., associate producer, senior editor)
- Contact details, such as email address, phone number, and physical address
- The beat of coverage (i.e., the topics they cover for that media outlet)

Review the publication's content and see what different reporters write about. This will help you determine the most appropriate reporter to approach. Always keep your target audience in mind. Knowing who your story is meant for will help make selecting suitable media outlets much easier. If your audience is comprised of potential investors or industry peers, then trade media outlets should be your primary consideration. If you are looking to be seen by potential customers, consumer media outlets are the best choice. Remember, you can approach both; you don't have to choose just one type. But the ways in which you pitch them may differ.

Media Pitches

After you've built your target media list and have selected the appropriate media outlets and contacts, it's time to work on your media pitch. In the simplest of terms, a media pitch is how we frame our stories to entice reporters and producers to obtain coverage. Expect to be rejected and ignored…a lot! It comes with the territory. When conducting media outreach, be persistent and stay positive! When you *anticipate* some level of rejection, it can be easier to handle. You will be sending out many pitches, and you should expect to send at least four follow-ups on each, spread a few days to weeks apart. Responses won't be forthcoming from most of them but don't lose heart. It only takes one person to listen, which establishes an opportunity for significant media coverage.

Everything You Need for a Killer Pitch

A media pitch is where you tell reporters and producers why you believe your story fucking matters to their audience. But to get them to listen, you'll need to know the basics of structuring a pitch. Before you start writing one, you'll need a proper hook to entice the reader. Think of the lead as the angle of your story and why it is relevant. Two types of leads are used in journalism and can be successfully applied to media pitches.

The first is a news peg. This is a trending news story that relates to the story you are pitching. The purpose is to hook the reader with current, relevant news. More on trendjacking later in the chapter.

The second is called a "time peg." This indicates an upcoming date or event. Anniversaries of special occasions or disastrous events (like Hurricane Katrina), or longer chunks of time dedicated to a cause such as "Mental Health Week" or "Breast Cancer Awareness Month" are commonly used to hook the reader with something current and newsworthy. These can easily be leveraged for PR purposes, and media outlets may choose to shape their content around significant time frames.

Tips to Pitch in a Nutshell

Your lead should be the first thing a reporter or producer reads. It should be attention-grabbing and relevant to their beat of coverage, otherwise, they probably won't bother opening the email, let alone read the pitch in its entirety. The next part of your pitch should be a call to action, followed by a value proposition. Your call to action should make your intentions clear, while the value proposition will showcase what you are offering and why it matters. The value proposition should differentiate you from the scores of pitches they receive. The final piece of the puzzle is the conclusion. This is straightforward, and here you can thank the journalist for their time and consideration and repeat your call to action.

Most pitches will be sent by email, and subject lines are often the first and only thing a media contact will see. Ensuring the subject line is written clearly and concisely will help to entice the person you are contacting to open the email. You may assume that short subject lines are best, but this is not always the case. Subject lines ranging between 60 and 70 characters have the highest open rate (Burstein, 2015). So don't try to cut down on your subject line length and avoid clickbait phrasing as this may leave a bad taste in the recipient's mouth. The last thing you want to do is appear misleading or spammy to members of the media! Some media pitching strategies can lead to greater pitch-to-press conversion, which I'll cover below.

Timely News Stories and Research

You are doing yourself a disservice by not using relevant research or news pegs as the hook for your pitch. The media lives on news pegs, new research, and trending topics and uses them extensively to tell their stories. Thus, if you want to increase the chances of generating interest in your pitch, make the reporter's job as easy as possible. They receive scores of pitches daily, so providing them with a story their readers will be interested in (as well as links to sources that support the story) will help to warm editors and journalists to your pitch.

Sample Pitch Letter that gets Press Coverage

Below is an example of an email we could send to media reporters, editors and contacts to pitch stories, interviews and campaigns for our clients. As part of our service, we develop personalized copy and outreach strategies around expert pitch campaigns tailored for each contact at every media outlet we target.

PRO TIP: The more personalization you include, the more likely you'll get a response!

Know the Beat

So many pitches are ignored because they don't align with the reporter's beat. Sending a finance reporter a pitch geared towards health and wellness is a blunder that blatantly shows inadequate research has been done beforehand. Don't be surprised if you get the cold shoulder in these cases. Whenever possible, personalize pitches and mention related articles that the reporter recently wrote.

Keep It Concise

An unnecessarily long pitch will hurt your chances of hearing back from the media contact. To improve your odds of receiving a response, show some respect for the reporter or editor's time and try to say everything you need in a paragraph or two, and have bullet points when appropriate. Be specific, tell your story, and point out how it aligns with broader media trends. In other words, offer the media contact value. The example pitch below details a story on remote working, but it still offers media contacts valuable insight.

Hi (Media Contact's Name)

I'm getting in touch because I came across several articles about remote work on (website name). I thought I'd send something your way that may prove useful.

My team and I recently ran a survey on remote work and found that remote work and productivity are two peas in a pod!

Here's an interesting tidbit:

> *95% of the professionals we surveyed said they got more work done when working remotely.*

> *In the survey group, 89% cited better work or life balance as the reason for this increased productivity.*

The research also dives into trends regarding the training of remote workers, how their environment affects them, and more. You can access the full report here: (insert a link to the source).

Would you be interested in using the findings for an upcoming article?

Thanks,

(Sender's name)

Following Up Is Key

As previously mentioned, following up on initial pitches is a crucial part of making contact. It is in the art of the follow-up that the most interest and responses will be gained, so set yourself up with some reminders to do so. The rule of thumb is to wait one week after the initial pitch before sending follow-ups. One week gives the media contact enough time to wade through their emails, but if the story is time sensitive, you can follow up sooner. Your follow-up email should include the original pitch at the bottom of the email to help jog the media contact's memory (Khalili, 2020).

Other Tips for Pitching Media

If possible, mention particular sections or columns in the publication for which the story might fit. Let them know if you're reaching out to pitch yourself for:

- *A feature story or profile*
- *A Q&A interview*
- *A news round-up*
- *A byline article (this is where you write the piece, and it is published in the outlet under your name)*

Reaching the Media With Press Releases

Other than pitching directly to media contacts, press releases serve as another avenue to reach the media. A press release is a document that announces something newsworthy about your solution. It provides all the important information a journalist or producer might need. Some media outlets will share your story based solely on the press release. Other times, a reporter might contact you to schedule an interview (especially if you regularly send out newsworthy press releases). Newsworthy announcements include:

- *Launching a new product, service, or business*
- *Holding a large contest, competition, event, or winning an award*
- *Partnering with a community organization, celebrity, or charity*
- *Sharing a compelling customer success story or announcing a merger or acquisition*
- *Rebranding of the business and the promotion or hiring of executives*

A good way to judge the newsworthiness of a story is to pay attention to the level of coverage other businesses (or competitors) have received. As is the case with pitches, media contacts are hungry for timely stories that interest a large number of people. These stories can have an emotional element or relate to current news stories. In addition to catching the eye of the media, press releases have several benefits:

- *They are cost-effective and can be used even if your marketing strategy operates on a shoestring budget.*
- *Press releases can be published online, which makes them good sources to attract customers, investors, and journalists, as well as backlinks to your website. When composed well, they can help to improve search engine optimization.*
- *Press releases can help you control how your story will appear in the media by sharing what is important and drawing attention to the value your solution offers.*

Finally, press releases make great content for your website's "news" or "press" page and your electronic press kit! This helps establish your credibility and gives you a more professional and polished appearance, making the visiting reporter's work that much easier.

Simple Press Release Format

Press release templates make writing in the correct format that much easier, especially since the standard press release is made up of seven parts.

1. A title and italicized subheading. The subheading should summarize the news you are sharing. Treat the subheading like the subject line of an email: Limit them to between 60 and 70 characters.
2. The location where the news is originating from.
3. Two or three paragraphs of details.
4. Bulleted facts.
5. Company boilerplate.
6. Contact information.
7. Finally, end the press release with "###".

Additionally, the upper lefthand corner should be used to indicate when the press release should be published. Typically, we use the phrases "For Immediate Release" or "Held for release until (date)" to indicate what is referred to as an "embargo." The consistent format of press releases makes it relatively easy for reporters to quickly spot the information they need. That's why it's important to master the format of a standard press release. Make use of a standardized template if you are unsure.

Press Release Types

Press releases should not be treated as a means of spewing a story to generate publicity. There are different types of press releases, each with its own formats and rules. Selecting the right type of press release can make all the difference in your marketing strategy.

Breaking News: The most commonly used type of press release. These releases relate to current news events, and the hook of your story is extremely important here. These press releases tend to be one or two pages long.

Product Launches: This type of release aims to highlight new products or product lines, pricing, availability, specs, and other information consumers may find useful.

Mergers and Acquisitions: If your business has undergone organizational change remarkable enough to warrant media attention, press releases can help you inform stakeholders about the goings-on. Details of the merger or acquisition are included, as are quotes from the leadership.

Events: These tend to be time-sensitive and give reporters something timely and relevant to chew on. They are useful in promoting an event and attracting more attendees. Make sure to explain the event details clearly and use bullet points to highlight the who, what, when, and where for readers.

New Partnerships: When you collaborate with another brand or non-profit, it can be a newsworthy event, and a solid press release will serve as a smart marketing tool for all parties involved. To successfully execute this type of release, you'll need to provide an overview of each brand and explain why you are collaborating and who is benefiting.

Rebranding: Rebranding comes with risks, as customers may be left confused if their go-to brands change their identities overnight. A press release announcing a rebrand can help to ease the transition and should include what changes are taking place, why they are happening, how they will affect your target audience, and when the changes will come into effect. Quotes from the leadership are included in this type of press release.

Executive Promotions: In larger companies and multinational corporations, executive promotions and new hires are treated as big news. Announcing changes in leadership positions will help stakeholders understand what is happening in the company. These are also referred to as "personnel announcements" and are perfect for trades and business journals.

Awards: Awards can help solidify your brand's reputation and credibility, so it is fine to humble brag about them in the media. Include details about why your brand has been chosen, what the award is, and information about the ceremony, if there was one (Hayes, 2022).

Techniques to Gain Media Attention: Trendjacking and HARO

Pitches and press releases are essential tools to help your story gain traction quickly in the media. Trendjacking, or newsjacking, is a strategy used by brands of all sizes to capitalize on trending topics, events, memes, and hashtags. It is a practice that helps brands build connections with their audiences in new and relevant ways. When done right, this strategy can help amplify the conversation around the brand and increase media impressions. To employ this strategy successfully, keep the following tips in mind:

Become Familiar With the News Cycle: Check the news a few times a day to keep an eye on developing stories. Tools like Google Alerts can help you cut down on unwanted screen time, as they will notify you about topics relevant to the story you may be trying to pitch. Signing up for HARO (more on this later) is a fantastic way to get the inside scoop on what reporters are covering, giving you a head start on emerging trends.

Be Patient: Just because a story is trending does not mean the topic will serve your purposes well. A trending story about solar-powered cars is hardly suitable for a brand that focuses on cosmetics. Be patient and keep an eye on the news cycle. Before long, you may spot something that will relate well to your solution. Trendjacking goes awry quickly when we are impatient and hasty, which can create unfavorable impressions on our audience as a result. No brand wants to be seen as tone-deaf or opportunistic, so when in doubt, it is best to seek the help of a trusted authority.

Act Decisively: The goal of newsjacking is to generate positive attention for your product and brand. If you hesitate too long on a topic, the opportunity may be lost. Trending topics are time-sensitive, so when you notice a relevant topic and have weighed your options, it is best to take action. Spend some time researching the subject, and make sure to explain why your point of view is unique. Being seen as an expert in your field, being quoted in coverage around the topic, or providing expert commentary in the media will do wonders for reputability (Le Vine, 2022b).

Trendjacking is a potent strategy because it meets the media where they are rather than trying to convince members of the media to cover a specific topic. It is a strategy that allows entrepreneurs to showcase what they are doing differently, while benefiting from exposure to a substantial audience. Remember that just because the media covered one or two angles of a story does not mean they are the only angles they are interested in covering, so keep an eye on the news and be patient! The perfect trending story for your brand will come along sooner or later.

HARO

Help A Reporter Out (HARO) is a result of how the Digital Age has advanced journalism. This tool provides journalists with a stream of sources for their stories and offers opportunities to those seeking media coverage. The platform is mostly used by journalists searching for experts to quote on a specific subject matter and can provide valuable press coverage, making it a veritable goldmine for PR professionals and savvy marketing teams. The pitching process is straightforward, and topics can be searched with ease, making it a time-saving platform. It's worth paying close attention to HARO, and the tips below will help you maximize potential high-reward opportunities. The best part? Signing up as a source is free.

Be Choosey: After signing up for HARO, you'll need to identify the topics or industries that align with your area of expertise. Choose these topics wisely, as you'll receive regular emails with proposed story concepts and requests for specific qualifications. Selecting your areas of expertise carefully will help align your brand with media contacts, outlets, and themes that will harmonize with the value you are offering. Focus on the topics that will most benefit your approach.

Assertiveness Is Key: Media contacts always have a pending deadline and need to work quickly to lock in sources for their stories. By keeping an eye on the HARO digests that come your way, you'll be able to act quickly when the right opportunity comes along. Most queries have a short window and expire in under 48 hours. Don't be afraid to send a quick follow-up directly to the reporter if you have not heard back from your submission.

Keep It Brief: As with emailed pitches, it is best to keep things brief. This is not the platform to share your 10-year vision for the brand or how many entrepreneurial milestones you've conquered. Keep your pitch brief and provide an attention-grabbing hook. Speak directly and use impactful words. Flowery double-speech and overly promotional or sales-y pitches are a turnoff for reporters and will harm your chances of benefitting from HARO.

Be Specific: Media representatives want answers that are succinct, direct, strategic, and trusting. The goal is to benefit from participating in a story, so keep in mind you are not the topic of a story yet. Honesty is the best policy.

Keep Things Relatable: By becoming a trusted source for media contacts, your story can find its way into media outlets with less effort, but there's another opportunity that the platform provides. The opportunity to connect deeply with peers and target audiences (Le Vine, 2022a). By sharing a touch of the human story behind your solution, a connection can be fostered with peers and audiences that can create unique opportunities that marketing and advertising can't provide on their own. A witty teaser will suggest there is more to your solution than meets the eye, piquing interest.

When used wisely, services like HARO open the doors for entrepreneurs and experts to widen their audience bases. You won't be chosen every time to participate in a story, but when it happens, you'll have an opportunity to share your expertise with the world, so craft your answers wisely.

Treating the Media as Partners in Storytelling

Cultivating relationships with media connections is important. In all that time you are not pitching to members of the media, you will do yourself a lot of good by fostering relationships with them. Don't misunderstand: By no means are we suggesting using others for personal gain. We are simply suggesting that you grant those you are pitching the opportunity to get to know you outside of the emails you are sending them. Building relationships with media contacts is not about being sneaky or manipulative to get your story heard. Not at all. It is about creating an authentic connection and building trust. Once a foundation of trust and authenticity has been created, chances are opportunities for collaboration that bring value to you and your media contacts will arise more readily.

Relationships are a give-and-take. People don't easily build relationships with people who only contact them when they want or need something. The same holds true for reporters and producers and is one of the biggest reasons why some brands struggle to get the press they deserve. Journalists prefer to nurture relationships with trusted sources (people they can reach for expert commentary, data, facts, statistics, and quotes for stories in a pinch) since it makes their jobs easier and more efficient. So, try to foster these relationships as much as possible. To become a trusted source, you'll need to:

> *Produce Relevant Content*: Any journalist worth their salt will do their research before reaching out for your commentary. You can't blame them for being cautious! The internet is filled with catfishers and pseudo-experts, so you'll need to bolster your credibility with a steady dose of relevant and educational content. Stay consistent with content marketing efforts as it will reinforce your status as a thought leader. This will help to

expand your reach, making it easier for media contacts to find you.

Be Honest: Dishonesty is a poison that destroys any relationship. Journalists must be wary of fake news, so before you share anything with members of the media, verify the facts for yourself. Provide proof for your claims. Misleading a journalist (even unintentionally) can and will damage your reputation and may end any future opportunities to gain exposure in the media. We once had a client send us a bevy of celebrity photos he stated were from his film premiere, which he asked us to quickly blast out to entertainment reporters. When we passed them through a "reverse image search" tool and located their true origins, we quickly realized what might have been at stake had we unknowingly passed them on as he intended us to do.

Keep Your Word: Honor any commitments you have made with members of the media and show consideration for their deadlines. Before accepting any requests from a journalist, make sure you can meet their demands within their timeframe. Tell the journalist immediately if you are unable to do so. They'll appreciate your honesty and consideration. Don't forget to reiterate that they are welcome to reach out to you at any time in the future. Your reputation won't be harmed if you are too busy to commit to a reporter's request.

Remain Patient: It takes time to become a valued and trusted source for journalists, so don't get discouraged. There are ways to help this process along, though. Just like you, journalists want engagement for their content. Follow your media contacts on social media, and don't be afraid to share their content and provide your opinion on it. In doing so, you'll help to improve your reputation with the journalist and your followers.

Most importantly, make the journalist's job easier! Assets—such as photos, videos, an electronic press kit, past footage of media interviews on TV, and footage from panels and speaking engagements—are valuable bits of content that will help to improve your credibility while making the journalist's job of crafting a story easier. Support your pitch by providing other expert sources for them to speak with who would help to substantiate the story concept. These sources can be clients, past customers, board members, investors, colleagues from your organization, or people you know from various associations. Essentially, these are people you know who could provide additional perspectives and quotes. Furthermore, make your media pitch easily digestible by using bullet points and distilling your STFM story into a streamlined and brief version.

The best way to grow your relationship with reporters is to see and treat them as partners. This means responding to their questions on time, following up assertively and politely (never aggressively), and inviting them to networking functions or lunch (if your relationship has progressed that far). Be patient and kind, and focus your efforts on building a relationship with media representatives well before you need them for press coverage.

Working With the Media

Before speaking to a reporter and going on the record, you'll need to make sure you are ready to work with the media. This means having a clear idea of what you are going to say and how you will say it. Once you speak with a reporter, everything is on the record, and anything you share can be published in print. Trust me, you don't want to be misquoted in a piece of coverage! Once that story leaves the journalist's desk, chances are it will live on the internet in perpetuity. Reporters won't revise their articles just because you asked, so the onus is on you to be fully prepared. To avoid potentially embarrassing stories, keep the following steps in mind when speaking to journalists:

Write Down and Memorize Talking Points: Your talking points are specific and clear statements you want to put forward in an interview. Think of them as sound bites, little nuggets of easy-to-digest and relevant information. These help to ensure your messaging is consistent and that you are positioning yourself in a way that you want to be represented. Take the time to revisit your brand goals and ensure that your talking points align with them. Refine and polish these talking points until they are perfect.

Respect Their Time: Time waits for no one, journalists even more so. Remember, they have tight deadlines, so pay attention to their preferred mode of communication and respond on time to their requests.

Ask for a Copy: Following an interview, you are perfectly within your rights to ask for a copy of the article before it goes to print. The intention is not to correct their grammar. It is a request to ensure that the content and quotes you provided are correct. This is what is known as an "accuracy" check. Don't overstep your bounds, as nothing will tarnish a working relationship with a journalist quicker than a source nitpicking over irrelevant things in the article. If you spot a mistake or have been misquoted, politely inform the reporter of your findings and provide them with the correct information. In most cases, the reporter or editor will be happy to make small changes as they want their articles to be as accurate as possible.

After an interview, don't forget to thank the journalist for their time. A little appreciation goes a long way in relationship building, and chances are they'll contact you again when the time is right. Journalists are always looking for the inside scoop on new stories, so sharing a tantalizing tidbit with them about future plans will give them something to remember you by.

9

AMPLIFY YOUR PRESS COVERAGE

You've done the hard work and have finally received significant press exposure... but now what? Stories eventually fizzle out and die, but there are ways you can milk media coverage for all it is worth. To do this, you'll first need to find your story. You've got to know where a story lives if you want to capitalize on it. These tips will help to make finding your story much easier:

Set Up Google Alerts: Use keywords related to your brand and story angles. This will help Google notify you if any links with the specified keywords show up.

Manually Search Media Outlets: Articles and interviews are often stored on the media outlet's website, so go straight to the source!

Make Use of Media Monitoring Services: This is especially useful if the story appeared on television or radio, as media monitoring services can directly source and send you footage

aired on local or national television or radio networks, sometimes even months later.

Contact the Reporter or Outlet Directly: Use the direct
approach to contact the reporter who covered your story. More
often than not, they will happily tell you where and when the
story was published.

Now that you've found where your story has appeared in the media, it
is time to use it. Publicity is a gift that keeps on giving, so don't be
hesitant to capitalize on the exposure you are receiving. As a basic
step, you'll need to link the story to your website. Create a section
called "Media" or "Press" and include the links to your placements
there. It may seem repetitive to link the coverage on your website, but
there's a good reason for this. Many people will likely miss the original
story when it comes out. By providing links to each story on your
website, you'll ensure that more people will be able to see it now and
in the future. Plus, it bolsters your credibility and allows other media
outlets to learn about you. Who wouldn't want to capitalize on a story
featured in *Forbes* or *The New York Times*? Unless you have explicit
permission from the outlet, stories that appear in the media should not
be reprinted on your website. That's plagiarism and can land you in
hot water. Links and screenshots are better and safer to use.

Use big placements for an "As Seen In" or "As Featured In" banner at
the top or bottom of your home page by including the most significant
5-10 media outlet logos (i.e., *Forbes*, *Rolling Stone*, Eater, *GOOP*, *USA
Today*, etc.). This will help with social proof and show the public and
other media the types of outlets that have covered you. These build
trust and credibility with your audience. Additional ways you can
amplify your press coverage are by:

- Including the coverage in your marketing materials for potential clients, investors, or other opportunities.
- Include press placements (also known as *clippings* or *clips*) in your electronic press kit and / or investor kit.
- Post press placements to your social media—LinkedIn, Facebook, Instagram, Twitter, etc.— and on your website's blog or Medium accounts.
- Frame great media coverage. If there's a story you are proud of (or if it appeared in a prominent publication), feel free to frame and hang it where walk-in customers can see it. Some restaurants employ this tactic when they receive favorable reviews from food critics. Get the story framed and printed by a professional, as it will be displayed in a public place and needs to look neat and presentable.
- Don't neglect the power that lies in word-of-mouth marketing. Mention it to others in passing, but don't be boastful about it. Some ways to use word-of-mouth include mentioning the article during introductions in a professional association meeting or in speeches where you are addressing a group (such as a book launch).
- Stories can be sent to your local newspaper if you've received coverage from national media. Chances are local media will be interested in picking up the story and may even run their own story.
- Let your alumni magazine know about the coverage. Most alumni magazines are eager for new information on alumni, so don't be hesitant to share your coverage with them. It may result in a small story or may grow into a larger feature article on your solution. Stories in these magazines can generate potential interest from fellow alumni, so don't let that opportunity pass you by.

Decoding the Digital Footprint

The story of Hansel and Gretel has a lot in common with modern business. Just as the kids leave a trail of breadcrumbs to follow in the story, entrepreneurs leave a digital trail for their audiences to find. A brand's digital footprint is considered to be the complete expression thereof online. This takes into account everything that's been said about the brand (like customer reviews on Amazon). Managing the digital footprint of a brand is closely tied to reputation management and is something that should be prioritized by every entrepreneur.

To get a sense of your brand's digital footprint, open a new tab in your browser and search for your brand or your products, services, or solutions. The results might shock you. The best-case scenario is that you've landed on your own branded content on the first page of search results. The search engine should have returned results like your brand's website, presence in directories, review sites, any articles in the media, and the brand's social media pages. If the search returns outdated information or if your content is buried six pages deep in Google's search results, it's safe to assume your brand's digital footprint needs some serious work. A digital footprint that works in harmony with the brand is a beautiful thing. If you don't manage your digital footprint, the internet might crowdsource one for you, and that is never a good thing. Fortunately, there are a few measures that you can take to increase your footprint.

Use Social Media Wisely

Social media can help establish a stronger connection with a brand's audience. Don't limit your brand to one or two platforms exclusively. You will want to be able to reach and connect with different segments of your audience. Different people gravitate toward different social media platforms. Any digital marketer will tell you that you need to be on the biggest social media platforms, but there's one qualifier: The platform needs to suit the brand and its message. Speedrunners are an excellent example here. These gamers dedicate themselves to completing games as quickly as possible. Some speedrunners break records, and others raise funds for a good cause, but you'll never catch them streaming the event on LinkedIn. You're more likely to find them on Twitch and YouTube. LinkedIn does not draw the audience that the speedrunners are targeting.

The advantage of being active across multiple social media platforms is that you can re-engage with the same prospects multiple times. Different people like different platforms and consume content in varied ways. Think of the difference between TikTok and Instagram. Both are highly visual platforms designed for snackable content, but TikTok is video-orientated, while Instagram focuses on images. By using different platforms, you'll be covering all your bases.

Use the Power of Email

Email is not dead! It is still an effective tool if used properly and allows you to nurture relationships with your target audience and media contacts. Additionally, email marketing can give better insight into an audience and exactly what they respond to.

Don't Ignore Content Marketing

Brands that tell a story that fucking matters are the ones that dominate the marketplace. This means that a mom-and-pop business can still carve out a reasonable share of the market by telling a more compelling story than its competitors. Continue to build your digital footprint through content marketing. Write about topics connected to you and your brand. This is also referred to as "thought leadership" or "authority building." Post to Medium, your blog, or your LinkedIn page, or pitch yourself as an expert guest contributor to select media outlets. All of this helps to continue to build upon the existing traction by including it in your marketing materials.

Optimize Your Website

Let's clarify one thing: a website on its own does not qualify as a digital footprint, but it is where the digital footprint starts. There's a bit more to creating user-friendly websites than heading over to Wix, Squarespace, or WordPress and creating a page. You need to make it easy for potential customers to find you. That's where keyword optimization comes in. Keywords are a pretty big deal. Search engines use keywords to find and display websites in their results pages, so if your website has not been optimized with suitable keywords, Google and Yahoo will have a hard time finding it. On top of this, websites need to be optimized to display correctly on your audience's chosen device. If your audience prefers browsing the web on their mobile devices, it will not benefit a website if it is filled with RAM-consuming features that slow browsing speed. Social media is an important component of digital footprints. It is best to link your brand's social pages to your website.

Build a press section on your website and include press placements and links to them in your press section. When it comes to broadcast footage, either create or consistently update your reel to include newer footage from TV and radio appearances.

Don't Go On Wikipedia Prematurely

Some businesses can get pretty carried away when trying to grow their digital footprints. A favorite strategy is to get their brand listed on Wikipedia. It's a sound strategy. Seeking a Wikipedia side panel to appear with Google's search results is a great credibility booster, but only if your brand is established enough. Wikipedia is pretty strict about creating new listings, and for good reason! A topic needs significant coverage from reliable, independent sources before Wikipedia moderators will approve the entry. Additionally, the page needs to be written by an independent author, and each cited source should offer in-depth coverage rather than a passing mention. In a nutshell, you need to earn press before you go the Wikipedia route. If you do not, you run the risk of your Wikipedia page not being approved for publication, or worse, flagged for removal.

Claim Your Brand on Google

A great way to boost your digital footprint and establish trust is to claim your business on Google My Business. This is a free tool that business owners can use to provide and update basic information about their business, such as the address, contact details, and website. The panel can normally be found to the right of Google's search results when searching for a business. One of the major reasons why you want to claim your business on Google is to boost brand visibility in local search results. Even if your website is beautifully optimized and discoverable by people across the globe, it may prove fruitless if your products, solutions, or services are not deliverable globally. Besides, most consumers gravitate toward local brands because they are accessible. Someone living in Boston might Google for a "coffee shop near me" or "Boston performance coach." That person is not expecting to see results that point them toward a Las Vegas coffee shop or a performance coach in Detroit. They are expecting local, accessible results. So, it's well worth it to claim your brand on Google. Your *Google My Business* page should be kept up to date with working contact numbers and websites.

Here is a bonus tip: Take advantage of free stuff. Find free listings and take advantage of them. *Yahoo, LinkedIn, Bing,* and countless others offer businesses free listings. These listings will help search engines find and recommend your business a bit higher in the search results, exposing you to new potential audiences.

Improving Your Digital Footprint With Content Marketing

There is a subtle but important difference between growing and improving your digital footprint. Even the most fervent content creators can have a below-average footprint. Don't be fooled by growing traffic numbers; this could mean your footprint is filled with keyword-stuffed second-rate content, which is a poor representation of your brand. When we want to shift our focus from growing our digital footprint to improving it, a few things need to happen.

First, you'll need to refresh any outdated content. Fresh, valuable content is key to staying relevant in the media cycle and helps build trust in your audience. You'll need a clearly defined content marketing strategy focused on answering the wants and needs of your target audience. In other words, tell a story that fucking matters and zero in on why your audience should care about your solution.

The goal is to become a thought leader in your niche through the content you share.

After you've created a snappy content marketing strategy and fresh content for your website, it is advisable to work back through your brand's messaging. Go back as far as you can and pay attention to the consistency of the messaging. Your audience will become lost and confused if the messaging changes abruptly, and it can lead to negative user experiences. Therefore, checking for consistency is one of the most important steps to improving your digital footprint. Taking stock of your brand's content and messaging is vital to uncovering what's working and what's not. Think of consistency checks as spring cleaning for your digital footprint: You can't give new content the exposure it deserves if old, irrelevant content is drawing your audience's attention.

The second step in improving your digital footprint is an intuitive one; namely, distributing content. How you distribute the content is as important as the content itself. Never distribute content that you don't want to associate with your brand, or content that clashes with your messaging. Next, you'll need to identify which distribution channels are the right fit for your story. To identify the channels of distribution that will most benefit your brand, you'll need to analyze your target audience and answer these questions:

- *Where does your target audience spend their time online?*
- *How does your audience conduct searches? Some people prefer to search using Google's voice search functionality, while others turn to their mobile devices. Knowing how your audience likes to conduct their searches will help you optimize your content for their preferred devices. Great content is useless if nobody sees it.*
- *What is your target audience's preferred method of communication? Knowing this will allow you to meet the audience where they are. If you have an audience that prefers email or texting, you'll need to tailor your message and adapt.*

As you chisel the answers from your target audience analysis, the appropriate content channels will start to take shape. For those just getting started with their content creation and distribution, it is best to focus on one channel until you've gained some traction. Nail down the nuances of your chosen channel and connect with the audience first before hopping onto multiple channels. Each channel, whether it is email, Medium, Reddit, Facebook, Twitter, YouTube, or LinkedIn, has a unique ebb and flow, so it is preferable to successfully connect to an audience on one channel than to have multiple channels that miss the mark. Distribution channels should allow your audience to engage with the content. If the audience is not engaging with your content, you'll need to revisit your content marketing and messaging strategies.

The final step in improving your digital footprint has to do with analyzing engagement. For this step to be effective, you should have experimented with different types of content (blog posts, videos, info-graphics, podcasts, eBooks, etc.) to determine what your audience engages with best. Track all your data-gathering efforts and analyze them once you've gathered a sizable amount of data. The data may reveal that your audience engages better with certain media, and this information can be leveraged to better reach them. This does not mean you should scrap all other forms of content! Not at all. Don't be afraid to try new things even after you've discovered what content types work best for your solution (Brooke, 2017).

There are so many channels to choose from, but the important thing is you prioritize quality content that offers value to your audience. This way, the quality of your digital footprint improves, and you can establish yourself as a thought leader in your area of expertise.

10

BECOMING A THOUGHT LEADER

Thought leadership is best described as original content from a brand or person recognized as an expert on a topic or industry. Business is not a static thing, and neither is storytelling. As businesses evolve, their audiences' expectations may change and mature. This means consumers will likely turn to brands that they trust. Trust is the operative word here, as it touches all areas of business.

Trust is the glue that binds both audiences and employees to a brand. Inside a company, trust is so important that it can even help reduce worker stress levels (Hall, 2019). From the perspective of trust, it is only natural that audiences flock to brands they feel have their best interests at heart. As a thought leader, you can help to facilitate that trust by showing potential customers that your brand is offering the solution they seek.

Brands that cut through the noise and have established themselves as thought leaders provide consistent and tangible value to their audiences. These brands make an effort to understand their target audience and tailor their messaging to attract positive attention. This means having an in-depth understanding of how the audience views the brand in question at different points of the buyer's journey. They take it upon themselves to provide answers to their audience as they draw closer to conversion. Once you've outlined the possible questions your audience may want to have answered, the focus can be shifted to nurture the value a solution offers for the audience. There are five ways to start this nurturing process.

Original Research

Original research can offer you the opportunity to promote your expertise and insights in a specific field. Identify key questions that relate to your niche and strive to provide your audience with concrete data that will answer these questions.

Original research also holds value for building brand awareness. Statistics can be cited in publications, used in tweets, or even referenced by others in your industry. This will help create valuable backlinks, which will help your digital footprint. All of this translates into better reach and engagement with your target audience!

Have a Point of View

Let's reflect for a moment on what a good leader is. Someone who shares their expert advice and opinions. Someone who people turn to for guidance. As a thought leader, you should strive to do the same. You want your audience to turn to you for advice and to trust your opinion. Therefore, you need to share with them your perspective and advice. Create content that shares your point of view on important or trending topics in your industry. Share with your audience why you reached a certain conclusion, what informs your decisions, and the advice you offer. When taking up the mantle of guidance, it is best to reference your evidence and credentials that support your opinion.

Your point of view should outline what advice you are providing and how your audience can use it to their advantage.

Keep Your Audience in the Loop

The Digital Age is defined by news that spreads quickly. Thanks to social media and the 24-hour news cycle, people have become used to regular updates. Therefore, it is only natural that people in your niche or industry also want regular updates from reliable, trusted sources. More importantly, these people want to know how these events or updates will affect them. Following this reasoning, you'll need to become a source of news and insight for your target audience to build yourself up as a thought leader. Your role helps the audience make sense of the latest developments and how this could impact them.

Create a Strong Cross-Platform Presence

Today's audiences are not limited to using a single platform. Loyal consumers follow their chosen brands on numerous platforms. Some prefer to receive updates in their emails and inboxes, while others prefer to scroll through the latest updates on their social feeds. And there are those who want something a bit more visual and readily turn to YouTube or Twitch. As a thought leader, you'll need to meet the audience where they are. You'll need to understand where your audience is spending their time and use that information to maximize your reach across different platforms. It circles back to the importance of understanding them.

Your audience may spend most of their time on social media at the start of their buyer's journey, which makes a strong social presence and top-of-funnel content crucial to maximizing impact.

Educate

A thought leader not only strives to answer their audience's pressing questions but seeks to educate others. In so doing, they position themselves as authorities in a particular industry or niche. Educating others can take many different forms, but most commonly through webinars, online classes, and podcasts. Consider for a moment how a student looks at their teacher. There is trust and an expectation of expertise from the student's side, while the teacher is expected to explain complicated subjects in a way that is easy to understand. One way to educate your audience is to establish learning opportunities for yourself. Whether you've found a novel method to teach English as a second language or created a Ted Talk on leadership, giving your audiences the opportunity to learn will help you gain a reputation as a trusted thought leader.

So, what is thought leadership, ultimately? It is those storytellers (brands) who offer tangible value to their audiences. These brands understand that their audiences want to learn more about their niche and strive to create trust while sharing their insights and understanding of impactful topics in the industry.

11

ADVANCED STORYTELLING TECHNIQUES

The degree to which your brand's story tells a complete tale is a predictive factor of success. Completeness in storytelling separates successful Super Bowl ads from the others, a finding backed by a two-year study (Quesenberry, 2015). Moving away from TV ads, a truly complete story involves a bit more than a compelling hook, a dynamic middle, and a memorable end. Your story needs to be implemented in all areas of your business. As St. Anthony of Padua pointed out in the 1200s, "Actions speak louder than words; let your words teach, and your actions speak."

Your story needs to be translatable so it can be implemented across all areas of your brand. Every interaction is precious, and every interaction should be geared toward bringing your story to life. Remember, in most cases, your brand's storytelling only has a few seconds to communicate the message and encourage your audience to take action. Consistency is key! This is why successful big brands and solopreneurs alike communicate their stories across all their channels. They create the impression that they are truly "living" their stories. Show your audience that you are actively advancing your story, and don't neglect the backstory. A consistent message resonates better with an audience, meaning more people will get why your story fucking matters.

Every element in your storytelling, from narrative to visuals and audio, should have a purpose. This does not give you the license to pull a fast one on your audience, though! People can tell when others are faking it. That's why it is so important that your storytelling comes from a place of authenticity and truly represents your solution. When your storytelling lacks this, the problem usually stems from either:

- *Your audience not understanding the "why" behind your solution*
- *Your inability to communicate your vision*

This is why laying the groundwork and leveraging the power of your emotions is so important.

Convincing storytelling is more than a compelling narrative. You'll need to consider how your message is delivered to your audience. Publishing your story on a website and on social media is pretty standard fare, so you'll want to think outside the box to grab your audience's attention.

A dairy company in Norway took its storytelling to the next level by cleverly using milk cartons to expand on an existing tradition. In Norway, Easter is the ideal time to binge on all your favorite crime content guilt-free. It is a nearly a century-old tradition and started in 1923 when publisher Gyldendal placed a front-page newspaper ad to promote a new crime novel. The ad appeared around Easter in the paper. The novel was centered around a train robbery on Norway's well known Bergen line. So many people mistook the book ad for a real story! When the truth was revealed, the book became a runaway success, and since then, crime stories have become an Easter staple in Norway. The tradition has been given a name, *påskekrim*, which translates as "Easter crime."

The dairy company decided to play on the *påskekrim* tradition by featuring cartoon crime stories on their milk cartons every time Easter draws near. Their audience loved the delivery method so much that they responded fiercely when the stories disappeared from the milk cartons one year. It was a case of "the tribe has spoken." Then they had to bring the milk carton stories back. The audience demanded it. The dairy company continued to offer *påskekrim* mysteries on their milk cartons every year since. They even took their activities online.

Fundamentals of a Successful Story in Action

Påskekrim worked so well for that dairy company in Norway for two reasons. Firstly, the milk carton mysteries are attention-grabbing and appeal to the tastes of their audience. Secondly, the storytelling method empowers its audience to become advocates for the brand. I'll illustrate this point with a likely conversation between two fictional coworkers. Let's call them Olly and Joy. They are both big fans of crime stories and enjoy the *påskekrim* tradition.

> *Olly:* "I can't crack this mystery."
> *Joy:* "What mystery are you talking about?"
> *Olly:* "The one on Brand X's milk cartons. Have you seen the latest one? It's a real doozy."
> *Joy:* "No, I haven't! I usually buy Brand Q milk, but I'll pick up a carton of Brand X on my way home."
> *Olly:* "There's a prize to be won if you can crack the mystery. I can't remember the details, but it's on Brand X's website."
> *Joy:* "Sounds interesting! I'll check it out."

Your audience can also become your biggest advocates. Encourage your audience to share their experiences with your brand through social media, reviews, testimonials, and other forms of customer feedback to create trust. Your audience is capable of creating a wealth of user-generated content that can be leveraged into authentic marketing and brand awareness campaigns. Some fundamentals will help you tell a convincing story.

Structure

Every story has a beginning, middle, and an end. It is a basic structure that does not change. The beginning hooks the audience, the middle provides a climax (a juicy reason to stay interested in the story), and the end wraps it all up. When establishing your own story, use characters and situations to which your audience can relate. This is where story kernels are handy.

Continuity

Storytelling does not live and die as text on a page. Successful brands tell their stories across multiple ads, channels, and formats. The secret is having continuity in your storytelling recipe. Continuity includes giving your audience a recurring slogan, logo, or character to associate with your story, making it easier to commit to memory.

One of the best examples of continuity is "The Most Interesting Man in the World" campaign for Dos Equis beer. The spots featured a debonair older gentleman and comically outrageous voiceovers. Since the spots first aired in 2006 in the United States, they have become a meme staple. Just in case you wondered, the actor who gave life to that debonair character is none other than Jonathan Goldsmith.

Relatability

This point can't be reiterated enough. If your audience can't relate to the story you are telling, then they won't care about your solution either. People connect with stories that fit with their lives. A story about life in the city might not be very relatable if your audience consists mainly of farmers. Likewise, a story about having children may not be relatable or even applicable if your audience consists of mostly teenagers or single adults. This is why it is important to know your audience. Only when an audience can see themselves in your storytelling will they be more connected to it. Stories are powerful cultural change agents when they give the audience something to care about.

Incorporate Emotions

Your audience remembers how you made them feel. By creating opportunities for your audience to connect emotionally with the story you are telling, the impact of your story will increase exponentially. We can find great examples of emotional storytelling in sports brands, especially where popular athletes defy almost insurmountable odds to achieve victory in their sport. Identifying what emotions your audience associates with your story and brand is a useful step. Place yourself in their shoes and consider what types of stories they might like to hear, and then use those insights to build a brand story with soul.

Local Stories Matter

The more locally driven a story is, the more relatable it becomes to the audience and their emotions. This is why successful solopreneurs share stories about themselves participating in their community. One way of doing this is by showing how your solution improves the lives of your local community members. For example, a performance coach might tell stories of a program they designed to improve leadership skills in middle schoolers and the positive impact it has had on their lives as a result.

Incorporate Novelty

It is easy to become so wrapped up in the details of your story that you forget to make it engaging. Stories can be simple and still get the point across, like Blendtec's "Will It Blend" campaign. Their solution, a blender, was on display for the world to see as they blended everything from phones to golf balls and other odd items. The tip we can take from their campaign is to leverage the power of novelty. People are mesmerized by seeing things or hearing stories that bring in quirky, eccentric, fresh, and funny elements. Showcase your creativity and leave your audience wanting more.

We successfully leveraged this storytelling superpower in 2012 when we conducted a massive PR campaign for a client who opened the nation's first-ever drag queen bowling alley, bar, and billiards nightclub in Las Vegas. Playing up Middle America's burgeoning fascination with drag queens, thanks to drag queen brunches and the mainstream success of *RuPaul's Drag Race*, our client quickly made national headlines everywhere from *USA Today* and *The New York Times* to practically every local TV news station, newspaper, magazine, and blog in the Las Vegas metro area. Within days, people from all over the world were flocking to this new club to see what it was all about.

Highlight Possibilities

Your story needs to show your audience how your solution will improve their lives. If your audience can envision that possibility for themselves, then you've succeeded in your storytelling (Marketing Insider Group, 2016).

Storytelling As a Call to Action

At some point in your story, you will need a call to action. The "call to action" lets your audience know what action you'd like them to take. The more information you can give your audience before the call to action, the better it can be implemented. Use clear and direct messaging to call your audience to action. Knowing what messages or industry-specific phrases your audience responds to is helpful in crafting effective calls to action. The tips below will help you to further refine and polish this call to action.

Use Command Verbs

You need your call to action to be concise and clear. Keep in mind, we don't have a lot of time to get the point across, as everyone else is competing for your audience's attention. Get straight to the point, and adjust your call to action to suit the storytelling format. If you run an e-commerce business, consider starting your call to action off with words like "buy," "order," "shop," and the like. When we promote newsletters or content designed to attract subscribers, the words "download" or "subscribe" are apt.

When we want to encourage our target audience to engage with us in some way (such as requesting more information), the call to action "find out how..." or "fill out the form for..." can be used effectively. Adapt your call to action so it aligns with your storytelling goal.

Let's go back to the subscription example. If you're marketing a newsletter promoting your latest financial tips and insights, you want to be sure your audience understands how to easily access that newsletter.

Note the difference between these calls to action:

- "My latest newsletter is available."
- "Subscribe now for weekly tips!"

An indirect call to action like, "My latest newsletter is available" is going to get you a muted, lukewarm response. Don't expect any miracles in the click-through rate either. When the call to action is indirect, it is relatively easy for the audience to ignore. The second call to action is much more direct and informative, which will help to improve click-through rates.

Use Words That Trigger Reaction

The goal of a call to action is to elicit a response from an audience. You'll have an easier time doing so if your call to action uses language that excites them. In other words, it needs to give them a reason to be interested in your solution. For instance, a travel agency's call to action might be something like, "Plan your dream vacation now!" In a similar vein, retail stores use calls to action to evoke excitement in shoppers. A bold call to action declaring, "Buy now and get 70% off!" is by design, hard to resist. This one points out the benefit to audience members and tells them how to obtain it, i.e., the customer needs to purchase the item now to get a 70% discount.

A small and effective touch is adding an exclamation mark to the end of the call to action. Exclamation marks convey a sense of excitement and urgency, and can help emotionally charge words, amplifying the impact of the message.

Look no further for a comical example of this in the iconic *Seinfeld* episode "The Muffin Tops" during the exchange between Elaine and Mr. Lippman surrounding whether to leave in or remove the exclamation point in the store's name, "Top Of The Muffin To You!"

Give Your Audience a Reason

Your target audience needs to know what is in it for them. Will your solution help them save money, find love, or lose weight? Knowing your audience's desires is key to creating a convincing call to action. "Call today for a free strategy session!" is a pretty good example. Not only did we state the action we wanted the audience to take (to make a call), but we gave them an incentive to do so (a free strategy session).

Use FOMO to Your Advantage

Fear-Of-Missing-Out (FOMO) can be a powerful tool to motivate your target audience into action. When people think they might be missing out on an opportunity that might not come around again, they are generally quick to hop on the bandwagon. It is a tactic that relies on scarcity. The scarcer we perceive something to be, the more desirable it becomes.

One of the best uses of scarcity in a call to action is to mention a sale or promotion you are holding. We receive emails with bold messages like this during the holiday season. These messages typically declare that a "Sale Ends Monday!" or we should "Buy Now While Supplies Last!" It's tough to ignore a direct prompt like that, especially when coupled with time-sensitive pressure situations (like the holiday season).

Get Technical

A killer call to action is dead in the water if it can't be customized to suit the devices your audience uses. Google essentially considers a tablet and desktop as the same thing due to the screen sizes and the way people use them to search for similar content. When we see an interesting ad on TV, we likely reach for our laptop or tablet to get more information about it. We are still in the research stage and are not quite ready to commit to the purchasing stage yet.

Mobile devices, however, have different user behaviors, making it prudent to tailor the call to action based on the device. Users searching for something on their phones are often looking for fast results. Think of the ways you've used your phone to search for information. You may have seen an ad on the side of a moving train and quickly pulled out your phone to search for what you saw before it left your brain. Statistically speaking, that search is also more likely to result in a phone call (Matrix, 2011). So, knowing what devices your target audience uses is helpful. For audiences that prefer using mobile devices, it is best to use a call to action to encourage them to make contact. You could try something like "Call Now to Get Started!" to guide the audience into action.

There are two ways you can tailor and refine your call to action even more. First, Google gives us the ability to set mobile preferences for ads. This designates certain ads to only appear on searches completed on mobile devices. The result? A call to action that can generate more phone calls. Secondly, call extensions can be enabled. This allows you to display your phone number alongside the ads. It is an option available for all devices. The best part is that Google automatically adjusts how call extensions are displayed on mobile searches with their click-to-call function.

Get Creative

Your call to action needs to be fresh, just like your storytelling. Some A/B testing is a great way to identify which calls to action bring in more clicks. Something may look great on paper, but we'll only know for sure if it works when we test it out. Your target audience may not respond to classic calls to action, so be prepared to test different versions. Instead of using "Call today for more information," try to spice it up. "Don't miss out! We're a call away" might prove to be more effective.

Use Numbers

Consumers tend to respond well when numbers like pricing, discounts, promotions, and incentives are at play. These numbers help consumers determine if it's worth splurging on certain items or services not essential to their daily lives. Try to include pricing information in your call to action if it is appropriate. If a member of your audience sees the pricing and still clicks through to your site, you've got yourself a valuable click and an increased chance of converting that click into a sale.

Use Negative Words

The direct approach is always best, but sometimes a risqué call to action can be used with great success. This can be tough to pull off, so use it sparingly. The author of a nutrition book might use "End your shitty diet today!" as a call to action. Yes, it might be a bit crass, but it commands attention better than "Improve your diet today."

Similarly, a garden service company might use "Your lawn sucks, but we can fix it" as a call to action. A consumer might chuckle or click for the hell of it to see what garden services they are offering with such a bold statement. When using this approach, keep in mind, you're walking a fine line, so it is best used sparingly.

Motivate Your Audience Into Action

Stories are great, but it will do you no good if you are rehashing any old story. To persuade audiences into action, you'll need to tell stories that leave them with lessons.

Great communicators have always used this approach. I refer again to Steve Jobs' commencement address at Stanford as an example. In this speech, Jobs told three stories with clear and applicable lessons for his audience. Similarly, Simon Sinek uses stories with clear lessons to explain his Golden Circle Theory when arguing that entrepreneurs should think beyond the practical and rational benefits of the solutions they offer.

Telling stories with lessons can feel like a tall task. You'll need to carefully consider the goal of your storytelling. Do you want to attract new support for a project? Grow your customer base? Introduce a new initiative?

Whatever the goal, try to think of it in terms of the following formula: *I want to convince A to do B so C can happen.* An author of a nutrition book might say: *"I want to convince single moms that healthy cooking can be a money saver."* The goal should point out how the reader will benefit.

Next, you need to think about the action you want your audience to take. Do you want them to rethink their views on healthy cooking? Do you want to encourage them to give feedback? The answer should be motivated and supported by your story. Let's apply this to the example we already have. To point out how healthy cooking can be a money saver, I would use a purposeful personal story. The operative word is purposeful. It needs to evoke some kind of emotional response.

Healthy foods are so boring. At least that's what I thought until I tried my friend's homemade pizza. I loved it so much that I wanted the recipe. She's a chef, so I asked her how much it costs her restaurant to make. "The ingredients will maybe come up to three dollars." That was the start of my culinary journey.

After you have your purposeful personal story pinned down, it is time to think about the relevance and lesson of your story. Does the story encourage the action you want your audience to take? If so, then your story is a keeper. Ask yourself: How is the story relevant to them? With our previous example, I'd say the story highlights a common perception of healthy food. Overcoming that perception is what started the author's culinary journey. So, by sharing something personal, the author is building familiarity and trust with the audience. Doing this also highlights the lesson (or the key takeaway) that the audience can save money by cooking healthy. So, if the author's goal was to encourage the audience to rethink their views on cooking, then it will work.

Motivating your audience into action is a skill you will refine as you continue to refine your storytelling.

Leveraging User-Generated Content

When storytelling efforts fail to connect with audiences, we need to take a step back and consider how user-generated content is applied. User-generated content (like comments and reviews) is a great way to show authenticity in storytelling and create trust with an audience. There are several ways to do this, but the first and most important step is to have a story that fucking matters. This might seem an obvious step, but without a story that matters, it is nearly impossible to take advantage of user-generated content. Give your audience a reason to care and they will engage with you more willingly. Once you have the storytelling pinned down, you can boost your campaign in a few ways.

Use Hashtags

A hashtag is one of the basic ways brands engage their audiences, especially if they are promoting on Instagram. Drive your hashtag campaign by asking your audience to share images related to your brand. Often, being featured on a brand's account is enough of an incentive to drive engagement. But if you want to create a nice buzz, consider challenging the community with a contest. All you need is a fun idea and some form of incentive for your audience. This helps encourage the audience to spread the word.

Speedrunners use hashtags quite successfully, especially when raising money for great causes. Take a look at the recent Awesome Games Done Quick speedrunning charity event as an example. The event managed to raise well over $3 million for cancer prevention by using hashtags and incentivizing its audience. The campaign had its own hashtag, and speedrunners and their supporters were encouraged to use it. On top of that, messages and shout-outs from viewers who donated were read aloud for all to hear. It was a beautiful give-and-take.

Collaborate

Social media is a wellspring of user-generated content. Here you can encourage your audience to show how your solution is used by real people. All you need to do is click that share button. Collaboration with your audience is a great way to make user-generated content happen, doubly so for membership sites. For membership sites to open the doors of collaboration, customers need to be allowed to share their ideas about your solution. Make a provision for a forum where customers can help each other and add a section where frequently asked questions can be posted and answered.

Reflect Interests

When we reflect on an audience's interests, feelings, and thoughts through our content, we are creating a connection. One that builds familiarity and trust. Every comment, review, and image posted by your followers will provide you with actionable insights into creating content that appeals to them—and content that gets shared.

Long-Form Storytelling

Audiences are more aware than ever before about social responsibility and the power their spending habits can have on global and social issues. Your audience has taken the time to research your brand, ensuring it embodies values similar to their own. This shift in behavior, where an audience is paying attention to social responsibility, highlights the need for storytelling to develop narratives and illustrate practices that demonstrate their core values. This means a 30-second ad won't cut it at times.

Long-form storytelling can be one of the best ways for brands to communicate their message. Take Johnson & Johnson's film *5B*. It is a documentary highlighting how Cliff Morrison did what no San Francisco General Hospital staff would dare to do: Find a humane way to care for and treat AIDS patients. The company commissioned the film in 2019 to show support for the international fight against AIDS as well as support nurses on the front lines. The film walked away with the "Entertainment Lions Grand Prix" at Cannes. The film was intended to convey stories of courage and motivation to find a positive outcome. In other words, it communicated the brand values of Johnson & Johnson to viewers through a memorable story.

Another example where corporate storytelling is designed to communicate core values can be observed in the "Rising Voices" initiative. This was a collaboration between Indeed and Hillman Grad Productions. The project was created to share stories about how jobs have the power to change the world. The stores were created by African Americans, indigenous people, and people of color, showing the world that the collaborating companies are committed to creating inclusive work environments.

Long-form storytelling can, therefore, show our audience we are invested in the solution we are presenting. It is a form of storytelling that gives us creative and narrative license to drive a point home and make that connection with our audience. Remember that your audience wants to be educated, inspired, and engaged. So, when the next ad campaign comes around, take the time to opt for a 20-minute explorative documentary instead. With the war, a post-pandemic world, environmental issues, and the "new normal" on everyone's minds, there are plenty of opportunities for solopreneurs and experts to take the reins and create content that connects.

Data-Driven Storytelling

It is no secret people love stories, and numbers can add richness and depth to them. When we make use of data to inform our storytelling, we've taken the first steps in telling an even more impactful story. Data-driven storytelling involves turning complex data sets into easy-to-digest stories our audience can visualize, understand, and remember.

Stories help people understand the meaning behind the numbers. This is vital because data is useless if nobody can understand or apply it. To illustrate the point: Jupiter is believed to have a diameter of 88,695 miles. That little dry fact does not help us understand exactly how big Jupiter is. If we wanted to make that data a bit more palatable, we'd need to say something like, "Earth can snugly fit inside Jupiter more than 1,300 times." It's the same data, just presented differently. A different angle.

Data-driven storytelling can take many forms. Infographics, videos, a series of founder stories, social media content, and even a billboard can form part of the narrative. The idea is to communicate the data engagingly and visually, just like we did with the Jupiter example. We used a comparison with something relatable to paint a picture of how big Jupiter is. The human brain loves visual imagery, so don't be afraid to use it. Our brains process images faster than words, which makes sense. The vast majority of information transmitted to the brain is visual. This is why infographics, images, charts, and other visualization methods are so useful in data-driven storytelling. They are quick to consume and provide convenient nuggets of information.

Journalists and marketers often use a visual format to present data—a kind of storytelling focused on conveying the solution or concept from a different perspective. Tower Electric Bikes took this concept and applied it thoroughly. They gave each U.S. city a bike-friendliness rating and displayed the results on a map. The result was a user-friendly image that allowed the reader to see at a glance which cities were bike-friendly. It was a method of storytelling that allowed the brand to showcase expertise in the cycling niche while providing value to cycling enthusiasts in a fresh and interesting way.

Data-driven storytelling is useful for brands for many reasons. The stories put the data into context, making it easy to understand the meaning behind the numbers. Data increases the credibility of your storytelling and reinforces your brand's status as trustworthy. Also, data-driven stories are highly shareable, exposing the storytelling to many others. It is a storytelling method that allows you to play with different formats and leverage different channels, so it is quite versatile, making it a boon for every entrepreneur's marketing arsenal.

There are three main use cases for this type of storytelling: Trends, comparisons, and relationships. Trends show how something changes over time. A cosmetics brand might use data-driven storytelling to show how the use of beauty products has changed over the years, which countries use the most beauty products, and what kinds of beauty products different generations prefer. All these stories are there, locked in the data.

Comparisons are pretty straightforward. We are using data to draw a picture, often with surprising or unexpected information that challenges beliefs. One example could be in showing the different types of beauty products Millennials prefer compared to Generation Z or X.

Relationships are complex, but creatively sharing the data can make correlation and causation much easier to underhand. Continuing with the beauty products example, the brand could opt to show the relationship between one's career path and their choice of beauty products or how skincare habits can improve confidence. It all depends on the message you want to get across. Telling a compelling story with data is doable, but keep these tips in mind:

Keep It Simple

When analyzing large data sets, it is easy to become overwhelmed. We can become overloaded by data and feel the burden of sharing it all. Oversharing is never a good thing in social circles or in data. Keep a little mystery alive and look for patterns and trends instead. That information will be most relevant to your audience.

Keep It in Context

Data without context is like a blueberry pie without the crust. It will spill everywhere. When we use data for our storytelling, we need to frame that information, making the audience understand the broader context. Numbers alone can't convey the full picture. Uber likes to use context, often comparing the distance driven with something relatable. Instead of saying, "You've driven X miles with Uber," they put the number into context with a comparison. This helps make the number more real by making use of visual language.

Picture It

Accurate data and fresh insights are important but cannot stand on their own. You need visually appealing content to cut through the noise. Sometimes all you need is an infographic or a beautifully illustrated social media banner to take your data-driven storytelling to the next level. Try to keep your imagery uncluttered and easy to read. If you feel unsure of how to create these images, consider collaborating with a professional graphic designer. They are trained in the art of visual communication.

Have Flair

Inject a dash of humor or put an interesting spin on your insights. Find ways to spice up the storytelling so it represents your brand's voice more accurately. Just because your storytelling is data-driven does not mean it should be soulless.

Use Storyboarding

Storyboarding is a good way to craft a compelling story and create a throughline. It can help you extract key data points and main messages, transforming abstract ideas into content the audience will love. Creating a storyboard is straightforward. You'll need to:

Prepare the Outline: In this step, you'll gather the data and extract key points. Ask yourself the key message you want to share.

Sketch the Outline: Start to sketch key messages into your storyboard.

Add the Data: Flesh out your story by adding the data. Think about how your story will unfold and put it in order. Tweak your story by adding missing points or removing redundant ones.

Add Visualizations: The last step is to visualize the data, whether it be graphs, images, a combination of both, or something else entirely to help the visualization make sense.

The most important part to consider when storyboarding is finding the data points and messages. After that, all you really need is the help of a good designer, and you'll be well on your way to telling a compelling data-driven story.

The human brain loves stories, so it only makes sense that we "storify" data for the sake of our audience. Successful storytellers use data to connect with others through unique insights and experiences. These storytellers know that facts present data, whereas a story gives meaning to that data. Content is king, but it is becoming increasingly difficult to capture the audience's attention. With all the noise in the media landscape, using data to tell a story that fucking matters may very well be the edge some entrepreneurs and experts need to drive brand awareness and engagement.

Storytelling Principles in Action

Disney is synonymous with storytelling and is arguably the first company to prove you can create a competitive advantage with it (Bloom, 2021). Storytelling is in the company's DNA, so it is no surprise they have wielded that superpower to its fullest at Disney World.

The park, which is about twice the size of Manhattan, shows us that storytelling is a vital ingredient for long-term growth. Upon closer inspection, you'll see that Disney World implements four principles to evolve storytelling into a high-leverage version.

Suspended Reality

Disney is famous for creating new worlds that audiences can experience. Maintaining an audience's attention has always been a careful balancing act. The key ingredient is impactful storytelling. Keep in mind, storytelling is not limited to words on a page. It is dynamic and multi-faceted. The Imagineers (in charge of theme park design) were well aware of this and applied it to several secrets of the park.

Disney World has spared no expense in creating a fully immersive experience. Under the park lies an intricate web of tunnels. The characters use these to navigate to their respective stations. The result: The characters never appear out of the world, and the audience doesn't see "duplicates" running around. Think of it as creating an immersive experience, but without the virtual reality headset. An out-of-place character would kill the buzz in that case. The Imagineers didn't stop at tunnels, though. The entire park is designed to have distinct kingdoms that remain separate.

Forced Perspective

Forced perspective is what makes some optical illusions work. Instagrammers use it all the time, as does Disney. Throughout Disney World, one can see examples everywhere; Cinderella's Castle being one. It has smaller bricks and windows near the top, creating the impression it's taller and further away than it really is when viewed from a distance.

Engaging Senses

Disney has taken every opportunity to engage visitors' senses. One such example is the "smelltizers." Smells and memories share a close bond. Certain smells can trigger certain memories, and the Imagineers were aware of that. Their solution? Hidden fans throughout the entire park that blow scented air. The result? Memories galore.

From purple traffic signs to era-appropriate bathrooms, many details are sprinkled throughout Disney World to deepen that feeling of being in a "magical world." Maintaining that level of immersion requires flexible thinking. Spaceship Earth is a spherical engineering attraction of beauty, and it hides a cool secret: It collects rainwater. The sphere's surface panels are separated by one-inch gaps that let rainwater run into the gutter system and lagoon. It is a little detail, along with others, that helps enhance the visitors' experience.

Sharable

Have you ever noticed how there never seems to be any sun directly behind Cinderella's Castle (or any other castle) in Disney World? That's because all the castles face north to south, which can only mean one thing: Awesome selfies! Stories are meant to be shared; they are pointless otherwise. The Imagineers knew this and created opportunities for the audience to share the story. By creating favorable lighting conditions in areas where parkgoers are likely to take photos, they increased the chances of the Disney story being shared. Colored concrete helps make the green grass pop and is intentionally used to enhance the appeal and appearance of areas in photos (Bloom, 2021).

The lesson any entrepreneur can take away is that the story needs to paint a complete picture, help others to see your solution differently, capture attention, and be easy to share. In short, if it is distracting, cut it out of your story. Reflect on your storytelling as a whole and identify any areas that can be improved to enhance the overall experience.

CONCLUSION

Tell Your Story…It Fucking Matters!

Every successful story demands something from an audience—that little investment of time. It is up to an entrepreneur or expert to make that investment worthwhile. Everything we do in business and in life has a narrative behind it. Storytelling is the art of bringing that narrative to life. We do this by sharing our beliefs and experiences with an audience in such a way that they feel it was created just for them.

Everyone has a story that fucking matters! You just need to fine-tune how you craft it and speak it. By mastering our three elements of an epic story—the *Roots*, *Stakes*, and *Impact*—your storytelling can evolve to grab headlines. Some of the most successful people in history have been renowned storytellers. Steve Jobs, Simon Sinek, and Aristotle all knew how to unlock the power hidden in stories.

Connecting with your audience through storytelling fosters brand loyalty. On top of that, it makes the brand more relatable, inviting, and memorable. We are wired to remember stories, after all. In a world where information is at our fingertips, storytelling helps us cut through the noise and build a relationship with an audience. When our storytelling is relatable, it strikes a chord with our target audience, and it distinguishes you from the crowd. Storytelling conveys purpose and is a strong business skill anyone can develop. The lessons in this book are aimed at refining that skill.

Today, it is exceptionally difficult to find success without good storytelling. Stories create context, provide meaning, and can evoke a sense of purpose. It all depends on how you use them. People are receptive to stories. That's why there's a growing recognition of the importance of storytelling.

Now that you know how to tell a story that fucking matters, it's time to go out there and be heard. We love to pay it forward, and you can, too. If this book proves helpful, help others find it. Leave a review. Share your story. We'd love to hear from you!

Visit us online today for free resources and to join our community:

www.StoriesMatterBook.com.

AFTERWORD

Danny Pintauro, Photo by Matthew Murphy, 2022

I was born in the public eye. Originally from Milltown, New Jersey, I was a Bicentennial baby in 1976 and was in a photo on the front page of the newspaper days after I was born.

Only two years later, I was modeling for the Sears Catalog, and shortly after that, I was thrust in front of television cameras to play Paul Stenbeck (Ryan) on *As The World Turns*. My formative years were displayed inside the pages and covers of teen magazines during my eight-year run on *Who's the Boss?* And around that time, I was interviewed by Oprah for the *first* time.

But I didn't yet know the power of my story.

I learned that lesson the hard way when, at 21 years old, I was told by the *National Enquirer* that they were going to "out" me. They were planning to tell the world that I was gay, and there was nothing I could do to stop it. As an actor in the 80s and 90s in America, this was a death sentence for an acting career. Everyone knew it.

Can you believe it? My own story was not mine. It was owned by some reporter in a cubicle trying to make headlines. Reporters understand the power they have but don't always understand the consequences of that power. And they certainly didn't care about removing my power from the equation.

I was in shock and felt assaulted and unprepared. I remember asking Judith Light, who played my mother on *Who's The Boss?* for advice.

She said, "Remember, they cannot misquote you if you give them the interview. As long as you give really responsible and mature answers, it can't turn out bad."

And she was right. By participating in my public "outing," I got the chance to help shape the story. The *National Enquirer* decided to write a respectable article because I gave them respectable and mature answers to their questions. I took some of their power away by being truthful and honest. However, they still got to determine when and where my story was told.

In 2003 I was diagnosed with HIV. I spent years worrying that another *Enquirer* moment was on the horizon; that at any given moment, someone would take away my power again and tell the world my status. I wasn't hiding. Most people I was close to knew, and I freely told those who I trusted, but—there's nothing like being forced to tell the world something very personal if you're not ready. So, I sat on it for almost a decade. And during that time, the stress and underlying shame tore at my soul and spirit every day. The stigma of being gay was strong, and I experienced the consequences. But the stigma of being gay *and* HIV+ was tantamount and difficult to grasp as the list of people who I could reference was very short.

Thankfully, no one took my power away over the years, but it wasn't until my thirties that I came to understand, thanks to Steven, that I could *partner* with the media to tell my story. I was in a great place in my life. I knew who I was. I knew I had my husband to support me through whatever happened, and Steven helped me understand the power my story would have if placed in the right hands. I decided Oprah was that person. She would be the proper custodian of my story —and I knew she would allow it to be on my terms.

Steven also helped me realize there was a larger story that I could be a part of—a mission to educate the public and reduce the stigma associated with being HIV+.

Steven is my friend *and* publicist; I knew Steven cared about this story deeply both professionally and personally. I knew he would be the right person to help take this story to Oprah.

It was a story he believed really fucking mattered.

In the previous chapters of this book, you've learned a lot about the process we went through to craft, mold, and get me in the right mindset to be sitting across from Oprah on national television telling my story. But this didn't happen overnight. There was a big gap between first approaching Oprah and her agreeing to do it, along with various things needed to converge for it to be the right time.

You have to remember that when you decide to partner with the media, you *also* have to be okay with the fact that there will need to be compromise when it comes to various aspects like the timetable, the venue, the scope, and the audience. Compromise is a good thing. If you stop compromising then you threaten the very power you were asking to have in the first place.

I hadn't initially sought to share my story on "Where Are They Now?" but I was able to make the decision for myself that it was the most appropriate program at that time, and I am so happy with the way Oprah handled it—with class, grace, and substance. Before the interview began, she simply asked me what I wanted to make sure to get across. I told her, we did the interview, and afterward, she said, "We did it; we told your story."

Not only did it feel like a weight was lifted off my shoulders when I finally got to share my story, but I have since heard from so many people expressing how deeply my story had an impact on them. For some, it gave them the courage to take ownership of their own stories. For some, it kept them alive knowing there was someone else like them. The ripple effect has been major. And I will forever be grateful for that, and I am proud to be "one of the first" to tell the world who I am on multiple levels.

I'm attempting a return to acting because we live in a very different time, and I feel ready. What a gift to be able to say I have no secrets from the world, *and* those secrets won't affect my ability to get a job. Progress.

Thank you, Steven, for your friendship, expert media advice, and all the years in between.

Always,

Danny

Daniel Pintauro
September 2022
Los Angeles, California

ACKNOWLEDGMENTS

Writing a book doesn't begin and end with words on pages. It is a culmination of many years, relationships, hard work, support and encouragement (and sometimes occasional ass-kickings), shared experiences, learnings, successes, and yes, even failures.

More than anything, books are about people. Where would any of us be without those who lift us up when we are down, teach and mentor us, challenge and push us, and love us (and conversely, invite us to return the love).

To Mr. William Shatner and Kathleen Hays: Immense gratitude for your kindness, loyalty, respect, professionalism, and support. Deeply honored to work with you all these years, and in support of The Hollywood Charity Horse Show, which is such a blessing of an organization. Keep up the good work in doing the good work.

To Lisa Loeb and Janet Billig-Rich: You are both absolute dreams to work with and to know. I am honored every day to get to represent you. That little teen boy with the Firecracker shirt is smiling ear to ear.

To Daniel and Wil Pintauro-Tabares: Thank you for inviting me on this incredible journey with you. From Oprah to Austin…and the next adventure! You mean the world to me.

To Souleye and Alanis: I stand in awe of your brilliance, creativity, intellect, curiosity, and consciousness. Thank you for your trust, support, generosity, and warmth.

Sylvia Allen: Thank you for your everlasting mentorship and guidance. Thanks for taking that call that one spring day and giving me a shot, and for all of your support all these years. So much of what I know I have learned from watching you, how to stand firmly in your integrity, how to market yourself, how to sell, and how to manage clients.

To Tony Scott and Joshua Rivedal for helping make this book a reality. And Team Grapevine and our cheerleaders over the years: Stephen and Nicholas Lucin, Laura Heckman, Anita Hyde, Ryan Paugh, Scott Gerber, Thom Singer, Sylvia Santiago, Lisa Schofield, Benjamin Trotter, Brandi Kamenar, Chuck Griffith, Michael Carbonaro, David Reddish, Damian and Marty Edmonson, Matthew Satterfield, Joe Stasi, Jim Christensen, Chris Beaman, Shannon O'Dowd, Maria Cifuentes, Ricky Londono, Renee Gannon, Alejandra Arteaga, Bryan Gonzales, Jared Haas, Paolo Presta and Patrick Thomassie, Andrew Pond Oldershaw, Mario Lavandeira, Duane Bates, Stephan Horbelt, Matthew R. Brady, Daniel Zahoul, Cyrus Webb, Janis Bernstein Schwartz, Ruben Diaz, Edgel Groves Jr, Chris Gardner, Rob Williams and Rodney Johnson, Yitzi Weiner, Monte Pittman, Lisa Claus, Jonathan Thompson, Christopher Ciccone, Josh Eisenberg, Michael Gutierrez, Kellie Elhai, Amy Lyndon, Justin Fischer, Armen David, Xiaofeng Gu, Priscilla Leona, Wendy Andries, Nick Petruncio, Andrew Davis, Jeremy Kinser, Andrew Warner, Travis Lane Jenkins, Donna Fenn, Lyndsey Parker, Pete Sveen, Michael Ciriaco, Jonathan Weedman, and Drew and Marley Slater.

And all of our clients and media who have and continue to support us all these years, thank you!

Steven Le Vine & Garrett McClure

Steven would like to additionally thank

To Dad (Marc Le Vine): Thanks for supporting me by taking me around to all of those used CD stores and record shows every weekend during high school, and spending countless hours in the living room transferring all of those concert bootlegs from cassettes to CDs. And for seeing my potential to become a publicist and shepherding me along the way.

To Mom (Betsy Le Vine): Thanks for unconditionally loving me, supporting me, and laughing with me.

To Grandma Sally and 'Poppy' Eddie: Thanks for teaching me about the importance of hard work, and how to become an entrepreneur and salesman at such a young age. I'll never forget when you told me not to ever sell items lower than their worth, but instead hold onto them as somebody later on will pay their worth.

Thanks to Sean, Winonah and Wesley Le Vine; Grandma Bea and Papa Larry; Aunt Candy, Uncle Lewis, Joanna and Seth Brown; Aunt Desly, Uncle Harvey, Uncle Alex, Bryan and Nassim Gamza; and the rest of our family.

Michael Beckerman: I would be remiss if I didn't take the opportunity to thank you for teaching me so much early on in my PR career. Everything I observed about how to successfully operate a company, lead a team, and provide value to clients, I learned working under you.

Dr. Lorra Brown: I learned everything I know about the practice of PR under your educational aegis. Thank you for seeing and championing my potential.

Steven Le Vine

Garrett would like to additionally thank

To my loving mother, Joanie McClure: your unconditional love and support fed and nurtured my eternally curious soul.

And to my dad, Don McClure, who taught me to read the Sunday paper: thank you for the love and all the lessons – many of which I'm still coming to understand.

Sunday morning reading with my Dad

To my brothers Curtis & Cullen McClure: thank you for standing by me through the tough times. It's an honor to witness the men you've become.

To everyone else who played large and small roles in my life: thank you for being part of this epic fucking story.

Garrett McClure

REFERENCES

Alviani, C. (2018, October 20). *The Science Behind Storytelling*. Medium. https://medium.com/the-protagonist/the-science-behind-storytelling-51169758b22c

Berg, P. (2022, February 4). *Using Social Proof in Marketing: Tips for B2B, B2C, and Non-Profits*. Forge and Smith, Vancouver Web Design Company. https://forgeandsmith.com/blog/using-social-proof-in-marketing-examples/

Bernheimer, L. (2019, September 26). *The Petrified Wood Principle | Psychology Today South Africa*. Psychologytoday. https://www.psychologytoday.com/za/blog/the-shaping-us/201909/the-petrified-wood-principle

Daniel Ellsberg. (n.d.). Biography. Retrieved June 30, 2022, from https://www.biography.com/people/daniel-ellsberg-17176398

BJ Bueno. (2019). *How to Create Strong Brand Positioning in Your Market*. Cultbranding. https://cultbranding.com/ceo/create-strong-brand-positioning-strategy/

Bloom, S. (2021, October 13). *High-Leverage Storytelling*. The Curiosity Chronicle. https://sahilbloom.substack.com/p/high-leverage-storytelling#details

Breakey, H. (2020, July 13). *Is "cancel culture" silencing open debate?* ABC Religion & Ethics. https://www.abc.net.au/religion/is-cancel-culture-silencing-open-debate/12449956

Brenner, D. (2015, July 22). *Storytelling Techniques: Opportunity*. The Latimer Group. https://thelatimergroup.com/storytelling-techniques-opportunity-%E2%86%92-leverage/

Britannica, T. Editors of Encyclopaedia. (2019, November 10). *claque | theatre*. Britannica. https://www.britannica.com/art/claque

Brooke, C. (2017, April 28). *How to Use Content Marketing to Grow Your Online Footprint*. Business 2 Community. https://www.business2community.com/content-marketing-tips/use-content-marketing-grow-online-footprint-01828696

Brown, K. (2018, November 2). *How to Write a Boilerplate for a Press Release in 7 Steps*. Fit Small Business. https://fitsmallbusiness.com/how-to-write-press-release-boilerplate/

Bullis, H. A. (2013, November 13). *Management's Stake in Public Relations*. PRConversations. https://www.prconversations.com/managements-stake-in-public-relations/

Burstein, D. (2015, May 19). *Email Marketing Chart: How subject line length affects open rates*. MarketingSherpa. https://www.google.com/url?q=https://www.marketingsherpa.com/article/chart/subject-line-length&sa=D&source=docs&ust=1660053136443721&usg=-AOvVaw0dgyUp6aMS-Gort_iyc_SnO

Bury, B. (2016). *Creative Use of Internet Memes in Advertising*. World Scientific News.

http://www.worldscientificnews.com/wp-content/uploads/2016/06/WSN-57-2016-33-41.pdf

Casad, B. J. (2016). *Confirmation Bias*. Britannica. https://www.britannica.com/science/confirmation-bias

Chen, J. (2019). *What Is an Information Silo?* Investopedia. https://www.investopedia.com/terms/i/information-silo.asp

Cherry, K. (2020). *Why the Halo Effect Influences How We Perceive Others*. verywellmind. https://www.verywellmind.com/what-is-the-halo-effect-2795906

Clark, M. (2020, April 30). *7 Organizations with Negative Brand Images and How They Overcame It*. Etactics. https://etactics.com/blog/organizations-with-negative-brand-images

Cross, B., & Richardson-Self, L. (2019). *"Offensiphobia" is a Red Herring: On the Problem of Censorship and Academic Freedom*. The Journal of Ethics, 24(1), 31–54. https://doi.org/10.1007/s10892-019-09308-z

Using story to measure and communicate your impact, and how to tell if it's working. (2021, April 21). Digital Storytellers. https://www.digitalstorytellers.com.au/using-story-to-measure-and-communicate-your-impact-and-how-to-tell-if-its-working/

Duarte, N. (2018, June 21). *How to Identify and Tell Your Most Powerful Stories*. Harvard Business Review. https://hbr.org/2018/06/how-to-identify-and-tell-your-most-powerful-stories

1890s – 1930s: Radio – Imagining the Internet. (n.d.). Elon University. https://www.elon.edu/u/imagining/time-capsule/150-years/back-1890-1930/

Epps, G. (2008). *The First Amendment, freedom of the press : its constitutional history and the contemporary debate*. Prometheus Books.

Fahmy, A. (2018, May 31). *10 Ways to Use Social Proof to Win Over New Customers*. Wuilt Blog. https://wuilt.com/blog/10-ways-to-use-social-proof-to-win-over-new-customers/

Forde, D. (2018, August 29). *PR In Canada*. PR in Canada. https://www.princanada.com/2018/08/29/what-is-the-difference-between-consumer-and-trade-media/

Digital Media Literacy: What is an Echo Chamber? (2019). GCFGlobal.org. https://edu.gcfglobal.org/en/digital-media-literacy/what-is-an-echo-chamber/1/

Gershon, R., & Smith, R. K. (2020). *Twice-told tales: Self-repetition decreases observer assessments of performer authenticity*. Journal of Personality and Social Psychology, 118(2), 307–324. https://doi.org/10.1037/pspi0000183

Goodwin, E. (2020, September 9). *The Majority of Americans Are Also Social Distancing from Politics*. CivicScience. https://civicscience.com/the-majority-of-americans-are-also-social-distancing-from-politics/

Hall, J. (2019, December 20). *Why Trust Is One Of the Key Factors in a Successful Company*. Forbes. https://www.forbes.com/sites/johnhall/2019/12/20/why-trust-is-one-of-the-key-factors-in-a-successful-company/?sh=fcdde8f59571

Hamby, A., Brinberg, D., & Daniloski, K. (2019). *It's about our values: How founder's stories influence brand authenticity.* Psychology & Marketing, 36(11), 1014–1026. https://doi.org/10.1002/mar.21252

Harper's Magazine. (2020, July 7). *A Letter on Justice and Open Debate.* Harper's Magazine. https://harpers.org/a-letter-on-justice-and-open-debate/

Hayes, M. (2022, June 20). *How to Write a Press Release (+ Free Template).* Shopify. https://www.shopify.com/blog/how-to-write-a-press-release

Hinckley, D. (2015, September 3). *New Study: Data Reveals 67% of Consumers are Influenced by Online Reviews.* Moz. https://moz.com/blog/new-data-reveals-67-of-consumers-are-influenced-by-online-reviews

Boston Tea Party - Definition, Dates & Facts. (2009, October 27). History. https://www.history.com/topics/american-revolution/boston-tea-party#:~:text=The%20event%20was%20the%20first

Freedom of the Press. (2018, August 21). History. https://www.history.com/topics/united-states-constitution/freedom-of-the-press

Hoeken, H. (2017). *Narrative impact: How stories change minds.* Stellenbosch Papers in Linguistics Plus, 53, 215–217. https://doi.org/10.5842/53-0-738

Hyken, S. (2019, August 11). *Unethical Marketing Destroys Customer Experience And Brand Reputation.* Forbes. https://www.forbes.com/sites/shephyken/2019/08/11/unethical-marketing-destroys-customer-experience-and-brand-reputation/#77a328da724a

Indeed Editorial Team. (2022, April 25). *What Is a Stake in Business? Definition and Who Uses Them.* Indeed Career Guide. https://www.indeed.com/career-advice/career-development/what-is-stake-in-business

Javanbakht, A., & Arakcheieva, M. (2020, November 14). *Social Media, the Matrix, and Digital Tribalism.* Psychology Today. https://www.psychologytoday.com/za/blog/the-many-faces-anxiety-and-trauma/202011/social-media-the-matrix-and-digital-tribalism

John Kenneth Galbraith. (1975). *Money, whence it came, where it went.* Houghton Mifflin.

Jurberg, A. (2020, August 17). *8 of the Most Costly Marketing Scandals.* Medium. https://bettermarketing.pub/8-of-the-most-costly-marketing-scandals-c4532da1b536

Kelly, M. (2016, August 21). *American History Timeline 1675-1700.* ThoughtCo. https://www.thoughtco.com/american-history-timeline-1675-1700-4076980

Keuilian, B. (2018, March 5). *How to Use Storytelling to Sell Your Brand and Vision.* Entrepreneur. https://www.entrepreneur.com/article/309628

Khalili, C. (2020, June 10). *How To Write A Media Pitch: Examples and Strategies.* Archer Education. https://www.archeredu.com/hemj/how-to-write-a-media-pitch-with-examples/

Klein, L. (2016). *The Anatomy of a Great Positioning Statement.* Thinkdm2. https://blog.thinkdm2.com/the-anatomy-of-a-great-positioning-statement

Kolbert, E. (2017, February 19). *Why Facts Don't Change Our Minds.* The New Yorker. https://www.newyorker.com/magazine/2017/02/27/why-facts-dont-change-our-minds

Kruger, J. (2015, October 7). *Did Danny Pintauro's Appearance on The View Help or Hurt HIV Prevention?* The Body the HIV Aids Resource. https://www.thebody.com/article/did-danny-pintauros-appearance-on-the-view-help-or

Lameiras, A. (2022, May 30). *Keeping it real: Don't fall for lies about the war.* WeLiveSecurity. https://www.welivesecurity.com/2022/05/30/keeping-it-real-dont-fall-lies-war/

Lazauskas, J. (2014, July 9). *Study: Sponsored Content Has a Trust Problem.* Contently. https://contently.com/2014/07/09/study-sponsored-content-has-a-trust-problem-2/#:~:text=54%20percent%20of%20readers%20don

Le Vine, S. (2022a, May 20). *5 Ways Tech Trailblazers Can Leverage the Power of HARO to Get Their Own Publicity.* Austin Technology Council. https://www.austintechnologycouncil.org/5-ways-tech-trailblazers-can-leverage-the-power-of-haro-to-get-their-own-publicity/

Le Vine, S. (2022b, May 22). *Council Post: A Quick-Start Guide To "Trendjacking" For Tech Disruptors.* Forbes. https://www.forbes.com/sites/forbesagencycouncil/2022/05/09/a-quick-start-guide-to-trendjacking-for-tech-disruptors/?sh=380c0d7d678f

Lesser, H. (2022, June 29). *Council Post: How To Leverage Emotional Storytelling In Your Branding.* Forbes. https://www.forbes.com/sites/forbescommunicationscouncil/2022/06/29/how-to-leverage-emotional-storytelling-in-your-branding/?sh=7ae763d5284a

Internet, social networks and VPN. (2022, April 22). Levada Center. https://www.levada.ru/en/2022/04/22/internet-social-networks-and-vpn/

Lyft. (2016, January 4). *Lyft is Closing $1 Billion to Continue Rapid Growth.* PR News Wire. https://www.prnewswire.com/news-releases/lyft-is-closing-1-billion-to-continue-rapid-growth-300198472.html

How to Use Storytelling to Engage and Persuade Consumers. (2016, June 14). Marketing Insider Group. https://marketinginsidergroup.com/content-marketing/use-storytelling-engage-persuade-consumers/

Matrix Media. (2011). *Outdoor Advertising Requires Distinct Call to Action.* Matrix Media. https://www.matrixmediaservices.com/outdoor-advertising-requires-distinct-call-to-action/

Markey-Towler, B. (2017, February 2). *How storytelling drives finance and economics.* The Conversation. https://theconversation.com/how-storytelling-drives-finance-and-economics-71813

Mehta, S. (2022, January 4). *Tech company Bolt is permanently embracing a 4-day workweek.* Fast Company. https://www.fastcompany.com/90710084/tech-company-bolt-is-permanently-embracing-a-4-day-workweek

Meta. (2016, April 20). *Capturing Attention in Feed: The Science Behind Effective Video Creative.* Facebook IQ. https://www.google.com/url?q=https://www.facebook.com/business/news/insights/capturing-attention-feed-video-creative&sa=D&source=docs&ust=1656934802887414&usg=-AOvVaw0ZYjyKtzjc-WSsEe1PQxMny

Moore, C. (2019, December 30). *What Is The Negativity Bias and How Can it be Overcome?* Positive Psychology. https://positivepsychology.com/3-steps-negativity-bias/

Murphy, R. (2019, May 21). *Local Consumer Review Survey | Online Reviews Statistics & Trends.* Bright Local. https://www.brightlocal.com/research/local-consumer-review-survey/

NarrativeIQ. (n.d.). *What Stories Do To Our Brain.* Narrative IQ. Retrieved July 6, 2022, from https://www.google.com/url?q=http://www.narrativeiq.com/what-stories-do-to-our-brain/&sa=D&source=docs&ust=1657107130128734&usg=-AOvVaw18e-D2dJ6CuHcNF0346uArA

Newberry, C. (2018, October 31). *How to Define Your Target Market: A Guide to Audience Research.* Hootsuite Social Media Management.

https://blog.hootsuite.com/target-market/

Newberry, C. (2019, April 17). *How to Use UTM Parameters to Track Social Media Success.* Social Media Marketing & Management Dashboard. https://blog.hootsuite.com/how-to-use-utm-parameters/

Nijjer, R. (2019, February 26). *3 Ways Social Proof Boosts Customer Acquisition & ROI.* Search Engine Journal. https://www.searchenginejournal.com/social-proof-customer-acquisition-roi/291903/

Nugent, A. (2022, April 4). *Is Inventing Anna based on a true story? Separating fact from fiction.* The Independent. https://www.independent.co.uk/arts-entertainment/tv/news/inventing-anna-delvey-true-story-b2050213.html

O'Quinn, K. (2016, August 18). *Importance of Credibility for Managers.* Td.org. https://www.td.org/insights/importance-of-credibility-for-managers

A Brief History of the Internet. (n.d.). Online Library Learning Center. https://www.usg.edu/galileo/skills/unit07/internet07_02.phtml#:~:text=January%201%2C%201983%20is-%20considered

Patches, M. (2019, January 17). *Netflix says Fortnite is bigger competition than HBO or Hulu.* Polygon. https://www.google.com/url?q=https://www.polygon.com/2019/1/17/18187400/netflix-vs-fortnite-hbo-hulu-competition&sa=D&source=docs&ust=1656957725316538&usg=-AOvVaw2ahih_JdFdM2AhhnICPQn6

How to Create an Authentic Brand Story that Actually Improves Trust. (2019, August). Neil Patel.

https://neilpatel.com/blog/create-authentic-brand-story/

Paul, A. M. (2012, March 17). *Opinion | Your Brain on Fiction.* The New York Times. https://www.nytimes.com/2012/03/18/opinion/sunday/the-neuroscience-of-your-brain-on-fiction.html?pagewanted=all&_r=0

Perera, A. (2021, March 22). *Halo Effect: Definition and Examples.* Simply Psychology. https://www.simplypsychology.org/halo-effect.html

Pressler, J. (2022, February 8). *How an Aspiring "It" Girl Tricked New York's Party People — and Its Banks.* The Cut. https://www.thecut.com/article/how-anna-delvey-tricked-new-york.html

Quesenberry, K. (2015, January 28). *What Makes A Super Bowl Ad Super? Five Act Dramatic Form.* Quesenberry. https://www.postcontrolmarketing.com/what-makes-a-super-bowl-ad-super-five-act-dramatic-form/

Ritchie, J. (2017, November 12). *Why and How to Tell Your Brand's Origin Story.* LinkedIn. https://www.linkedin.com/business/marketing/blog/content-marketing/why-you-should-tell-your-brand-s-origin-story-and-how-to-do-it

Romano, J. (2021, September 23). *How to Create a Brand Positioning Strategy for Your Business.* Wix Blog. https://www.wix.com/blog/2021/09/brand-positioning-strategy/

Roose, K. (2018, October 28). *On Gab, an Extremist-Friendly Site, Pittsburgh Shooting Suspect Aired His Hatred in Full.* The New York Times. https://www.nytimes.com/2018/10/28/us/gab-robert-bowers-pittsburgh-synagogue-shootings.html

Roth, G. (n.d.). *5 Real-World Examples of Authentic Social Proof to Boost Sales.* Growth Leap. Retrieved July 14, 2022, from https://www.growthleap.com/blog/5-real-world-examples-of-authentic-social-proof-to-boost-sales/

Sehl, K. (2019, February 5). *How to Use Facebook Lookalike Audiences: The Complete Guide.* Social Media Marketing & Management Dashboard. https://blog.hootsuite.com/facebook-lookalike-audiences/

Seitz, A., & Klepper, D. (2022, February 24). *Propaganda, fake videos of Ukraine invasion bombard users.* AP NEWS. https://apnews.com/article/russia-ukraine-technology-europe-media-social-media-80f729025396abf9ad9e4e9d0b4f5ece

Severin, K. (2019, February 12). *Major Games Publishers Are Feeling The Impact Of Peaking Attention.* MIDiA Research. https://www.midiaresearch.com/blog/major-games-publishers-are-feeling-the-impact-of-peaking-attention/

Stephen, B. (2019, March 3). *The attention economy is dead.* The Verge. https://www.theverge.com/2019/3/3/18246868/attention-economy-fortnite-advertising-user-engagement

Stephens, G. J., Silbert, L. J., & Hasson, U. (2010). *Speaker-listener neural coupling underlies successful communication.* Proceedings of the National Academy of Sciences, 107(32), 14425–14430. https://doi.org/10.1073/pnas.1008662107

Creating bonds with viewer-centric video. (2019). Think with Google. https://www.thinkwithgoogle.com/intl/en-154/marketing-strategies/video/gant-creates-stronger-bonds-their-target-audience-through-viewer-centric-youtube-content/

Walters, D., & White, D. (1987). *Merchandise Management: Marketing Considerations.* Retail Marketing Management, 119–138. https://doi.org/10.1007/978-1-349-10666-0_6

Wigmore, I. (2019, June). *What is information overload?* What Is. https://www.techtarget.com/whatis/definition/information-overload#:~:text=Information%20overload%20is%20a%20state

Uncle Tom. (2019a, March 24). Wikimedia Foundation. https://en.wikipedia.org/wiki/Uncle_Tom

Echo chamber (media). (2019b, August 8). Wikimedia Foundation. https://en.wikipedia.org/wiki/Echo_chamber_(media)

Broadcasting in the United States. (2021, December 22). Wikipedia.

https://en.wikipedia.org/wiki/Broadcasting_in_the_United_States

History of newspaper publishing. (2022, June 30). Wikipedia. https://en.m.wikipedia.org/wiki/History_of_newspaper_publishing

Woods, H., & Hahner, L. (2018, November 30). *How mainstream media helps weaponize far-right conspiracy theories.* The Conversation. https://theconversation.com/how-mainstream-media-helps-weaponize-far-right-conspiracy-theories-106223